Understanding the
CREATION
EVOLUTION
Controversy

A Scientific Evaluation Consistent with Both
Modern Science and the Bible

E.C. A S H B Y, Ph.D.

ACW Press
Ozark, AL 36360

Understanding the Creation/Evolution Controversy
Copyright ©2005 E.C. Ashby, Ph.D.
All rights reserved

Front cover photo of the Eta Carinea nebula is by Bob Sandness
Cover Design by Alpha Advertising
Interior Design by Pine Hill Graphics

Packaged by ACW Press
1200 HWY 231 South #273
Ozark, AL 36360
www.acwpress.com
The views expressed or implied in this work do not necessarily reflect those of ACW
Press. Ultimate design, content, and editorial accuracy of this work is the responsibility
of the author(s).

Library of Congress Cataloging-in-Publication Data
(Provided by Cassidy Cataloguing Services, Inc.)

Ashby, E. C.

    Understanding the creation controversy : a scientific evaluation
    consistent with both modern science and the Bible / E. C. Ashby. --
    1st ed. -- Ozark, AL : ACW Press, 2005.

      p. ; cm.
      ISBN: 1-932124-56-X

    1. Creationism. 2. Evolution. 3. Bible and evolution. 4. Evolution
    (Biology)--Religious aspects--Christianity. I. Title.

BS651 .A83 2005
231.7/652--dc22   0504

Printed in the United States of America.

This book is dedicated to the memory of Frank Elliott who died June 25, 2002, at the age of 92. People have complained that the trouble with the world today is that it has no heroes. The truth is that the world is filled with heroes and Frank Elliot was just one of the best examples.

Table of Contents

Note to the Reader

IT SEEMS THAT IF YOU ASK MOST CHRISTIANS TODAY IF THEY believe in evolution, they would say no! This response is because of what they have heard others say and, in addition, they believe that evolution is against the teachings of the Bible. The question of evolution is important enough for Christians to study the issues carefully and come to an informed position as to its merits. This writer is a committed Christian who believes that the Bible is the inspired Word of God and reads from its pages daily. Therefore, if I render an opinion about evolution, creationists cannot say the opinion comes from a godless atheist. Likewise, I am considered to be a distinguished scientist. Therefore, if I render an opinion about creation, evolutionists cannot say that this is another opinion of an uninformed and uneducated Christian.

This book is not meant to be a detailed scientific analysis of the creation/evolution controversy written for readers with a strong scientific background. Such a book might be 600 pages in length and could be read and understood only by a relatively small audience. On the contrary, it is meant to be a simple and concise analysis of the creation/evolution controversy, written so that the average educated layperson could arrive at a reasonable understanding of this complicated subject.

I have spent five years researching and writing this book; the conclusions come from a writer who is committed to the truth and who has not been influenced by previous pronouncements on either side of the creation/evolution controversy.

Acknowledgements

I AM TREMENDOUSLY GRATEFUL TO THE REVIEWERS OF THIS book. They include a Nobel Prize winner in chemistry; a former president of the American Chemical Society; a molecular biologist, three biochemists, a chemist, a geologist, a microbiologist, a high school biology teacher and a publisher of high school textbooks.

The reviewers are: H.C. Brown; R.B. Wetherill, professor of Chemistry emeritus, Purdue University; Ernest Eliel, Keenan professor of Chemistry emeritus, University of North Carolina, Chapel Hill; Paul Anderson, professor emeritus, Department of Biochemistry and Molecular Biology, School of Medicine, University of Minnesota, Duluth; Drury Caine, professor emeritus, Department of Chemistry, University of Alabama; James Powers, Regents' professor, School of Chemistry and Biochemistry, Georgia Institute of Technology; Richard W. Ojakangas, professor emeritus, Department of Geological Sciences, University of Minnesota, Duluth; Howard Deutsch, professor of chemistry, School of Chemistry and Biochemistry, Georgia Institute of Technology; David Mudd, biology teacher, South Gwinnett High School, Atlanta, Georgia; Kevin Redding, assistant professor, Department of Chemistry, University of Alabama; Chris Learn, associate in research, Department of Surgery, Duke University Medical Center; and Bruce Cook, president, Choosing the Best Publishing Company, Atlanta, Georgia.

All of the reviewers have made detailed, pertinent comments and have asked many penetrating questions. Although I was not able to satisfy all of the criticisms presented by the reviewers, this book is definitely better for my attempt to do so. These reviewers should not be held accountable for any inaccuracies in this book, but rather complimented on their efforts to make the book better.

I am also extremely grateful to the love of my life, my wife Carolyn, for her patience and understanding during this and many other projects. In addition, I am also deeply grateful to Ms. Mary Ellen Johnson and Ms. Angela Whitfield for typing this manuscript, for their patience and their helpful suggestions. Most of all I am deeply grateful to a gracious and merciful God who has inspired me and more than helped me to write this book.

Preface

WHEN I WAS SIXTEEN YEARS OLD I ATTENDED A LECTURE AT Tulane University given by the famous physicist George Gamow. He introduced to the audience the "big bang" theory to describe the origin of the universe. It has been 55 years since this lecture, but I still remember clearly that Dr. Gamow was a big man with a high-pitched voice who made the universe come alive as an exquisitely beautiful and mathematically accurate conglomeration of stars and planets, nebulae and galaxies.

My interest in the origin of the universe began with that lecture; nevertheless, I did not spend my professional life in astronomy, but in chemistry. However, after retirement from 30 years of teaching and research at Georgia Tech, the flame of my old interest in the universe was rekindled. This rekindling process took place in the form of a book by Hugh Ross entitled *The Creator and the Cosmos*, sent to me by a good friend, Frank Elliott. This exciting book was planted in fertile ground because of my interest in the creation/evolution controversy that has generated so much emotional debate over such a long period of time. I thought surely there must be a rational answer to this conflict, if one would take sufficient time to study both sides of the question. After some time I came to the realization that I should do such a study and, if successful in coming to a clear understanding, to record these findings— not in a detailed way for scientists, but in a more general way for the nonscientifically trained person. Although I had no formal training in astronomy or molecular biology, I decided to make an all-out effort to educate myself in these disciplines in order to address the areas of the origin of the universe, the origin of life, and the origin of man. My background involving 45 years in chemistry served me well in this effort.

For two years I studied diligently, full time, by reading everything I could find on the above subjects. Then I spent the next three years writing, editing and rethinking all conclusions before the final copy of this book. My efforts were mainly in the areas of astronomy, anthropology, biology, biochemistry and molecular biology. Although I read quite a number of books and many articles, I approached the study in a completely open, but intense, systematic and objective fashion as I had done many times before in difficult research projects. I had hoped that a clear and broad picture would emerge from the multitude of opinions and overwhelming amounts of data that I had collected from numerous contributors. Indeed, I feel that a reasonably clear picture has emerged.

In all of the reading that I did, the greatest help I received in the area of the origin of the universe came from the scholarly writings of Hugh Ross, not only his books, but also his newsletters, *Facts and Faith* and *Connections*. His first book, *The Creator and the Cosmos*, is incredibly informative and is a good introduction to the origin of the universe. Four other books written by him—*The Fingerprint of God, Creation and Time, Beyond the Cosmos* and *The Genesis Question*—are also excellent. Other helpful books concerning the origin of the universe are *The Science of God* by Gerald Schroeder and *Genesis One and the Origin of the Earth* by Robert C. Newman and Herman J Eckelman, Jr.

For me the most informative book concerning the Origin of Life is the amazingly broad and informative book by Michael Denton entitled *Evolution: A Theory in Crisis*. Later, Michael J. Behe's book, *Darwin's Black Box*, appeared which focused on the principle of irreducible complexity and provided a strong basis for the theory of intelligent design. Other books by Philip E. Johnson entitled *Defeating Darwinism* and *Darwin on Trial*, a book by Charles B. Thaxton, Walter L. Bradley and Roger L. Olsen entitled *The Mystery of Life's Origin* and a book by Alan Haywood entitled *Creation and Evolution* are also exceptional. Johnson's books, published in 1991 and 1997, provided an early, broad and challenging understanding of what was known about the creation/evolution controversy from a creationist's perspective. The impact of Johnson's books cannot be overemphasized as to their effect in encouraging many other contributors that followed. The latter two books by Thaxton et al. and Haywood deal mainly with the chemistry of life and are very important contributions.

There are, of course, many books dealing with evolution and the origin of man. An initial introduction might best be obtained from a high school biology text such as *Biology*, by Miller and Levine (in particular, chapters 5,7,9,10,13,14,16 and 34) and a thorough reading of Michael Denton's book entitled *Evolution: A Theory in Crisis*. After this introduction, five books are highly recommended: *Finding Darwin's God* by Kenneter R. Miller, *The Triumph of Evolution and the Failure of Creationism* by Nick Eldridge, *Wonderful Life, The Burgess Shale and the Nature of History* by Stephen J. Gould, *Molecular Biology of the Cell* by Bruce Alberts et al. and *Culture, People, Nature: An Introduction to General Anthropology* by Marvin Harris. I am very grateful to all of the scientists whose papers and books I have read in order to arrive at the level of understanding necessary to write this book.

After studying in the area of anthropology, which I found extremely interesting but not as scientifically demanding as the physical sciences (chemistry, physics and biology), it became apparent to me that the question as to whether or not man's origin is that of a common ancestor of the ape was extremely complex, and indeed is not knowable with any certainty at this time. However, what is even a more important question is not the origin of man, but the origin of life. Since Darwinian evolution maintains that all species proceeded from a previous species by a gradual process of change, and eventually from the same single cell, it became apparent that the more revealing question is not the origin of man, but rather the origin of the first cell from which man was said to have originated. Is it possible that the first cell could have come about by chance or was it necessary to invoke the principle of intelligent design (creation by God)? Additionally, the question is, where did the thousands of proteins, enzymes, carbohydrates, lipids etc., that are found in a human cell originate? We have carried out a number of probability calculations concerning the formation of certain enzymes and proteins and have determined that it is highly improbable, if not impossible, that even one enzyme could form by chance, much less 2,000 enzymes and thousands of other proteins, carbohydrates, lipids, DNA, RNA, etc., that are the essential components of a cell. What kind of explanation could one propose for the formation of such compounds, plus the operation of thousands of stereospecific biological reactions defining the molecular biology and physiology of the human body? The most logical answer is intelligent design, but does this answer hold up to scientific scrutiny?

There are several objectives that have been pursued in writing this book. The first objective is to present a scientific evaluation of what is known about the origin of the universe and to state the reasonableness of such an evaluation to support the big bang theory. In addition, an attempt is made to provide evidence for a 17 billion year old universe and a 4 billion year old earth, and to show that the big bang theory is not contrary to biblical teaching. This position, of course, is in direct opposition to the position of scientific creationism which holds that the earth is 6,000-10,000 years old and that all creation took place during a six 24-hour day creation period. The second purpose of this book is to show that the present thinking concerning the evolution of man has been somewhat distorted by false or invalid accounts of fossil findings and certain anomalous observations. This is not to say that the scientific basis for the evolution of man is completely in error, but that the initial general acceptance of the theory of Darwinian evolution was based on many false or misleading reports. The third purpose of this book is to reduce the argument concerning the origin of life from one involving anthropology, paleontology and the age of the earth, to an argument involving the mathematical probability of initiating life by chance through the formation of biologically active molecules formed at random in a primordial soup. In addition, it would be important to address the probability of producing biological and physiological processes dictated by the information contained in the chromosomes, as well as how did such specific and complex information get encoded in the chromosomes? And finally, it would be important to arrive at a clear understanding of the relationship of the origin of the universe, the origin of life and the origin of man and how these origins relate to the creation/evolution controversy. The question then is, did the universe and life come about by chance or were they the result of creation?

The most controversial of all of the areas studied is that which relates to the origin of man and his proposed evolution from a common ancestor of the ape. The results of our studies do shed some light on the confusion. Biology does provide strong evidence that one species can evolve into another species that is similar in morphology and DNA (microevolution). On the other hand, there is much less evidence to support the general theory (Darwinian evolution) that all species evolved through the evolutionary process: single cell, kingdom, phylum, class, order, family, genus, species (macroevolution). However, and more importantly, biology cannot account for the initiation of life by the formation of a single cell. This dilemma suggests a logical proposal concerning the origin of life and that is due to an act by a "super intellect" as suggested earlier by Einstein and Hawking to explain the origin of the universe. Although Einstein and Hawking did not believe in a personal God, many believe, with evidence, that this super intellect is the God of the Bible. Indeed, there is considerable scientific evidence in the areas of astronomy, anthropology, biochemistry, molecular biology and physiology that does point to the origin of the universe and the origin of life as a creative act by a supernatural Being.

As mentioned earlier, this book was written to be understood by the average educated, but not scientifically trained, person. Even more specifically, it was written for twelfth grade – first year college students in order to put in perspective the much-confused area of creation/evolution so that students are not overwhelmed with the common misconceptions about the origin of the universe and the origin of life to which they have been and will be further exposed. Since the theory of creation is not allowed to be discussed in the classrooms of our country, I hope that this book will serve to present a rational and objective scientific discussion of this topic for all students.

In some places in this book the scientific material may seem too complicated to understand. However, the reader does not have to understand in-depth the specific chemistry or astronomy being presented, but simply grasp the general idea of the complex situations. If the origins of the universe and life are believed to be impossible by chance, it is because the processes used to explain the formation of the universe and life are much too complicated to have just happened without any direction. Therefore, the complexity of some of these processes must be presented in order to give the reader the opportunity to see that such complex processes could not come about by chance. Nevertheless, I have made every effort to keep this book concise and not go into too much detail in order to keep it easily readable.

What the following discussion will show is that the universe and life are the result of creation followed by evolution. For example, it will become clear that the origin of the universe was the result of a creative act (the "big bang") 17 billion years ago and that the universe has continued to evolve (gradually change) to its present state. Likewise, all evidence considered here points to the proposition that life (the first cell) originated as the result of a creative act, followed by the creation of plant life, marine life and birds, land animals and man, with new species appearing as a result of microevolution, or limited macroevolution. Also it is suggested that the greatest impediment to accepting the theory of Darwinian evolution has been the discovery of the Burgess Shale which shows that major units of life (phylum) came about abruptly during the Cambrian Explosion 540 million years ago and not gradually as proposed by Darwin.[1]

Indeed, the phenomenological process of evolution certainly does propose a reasonable hypothesis for the appearance of many new species originating from the 70 phyla which appeared at the time of the Cambrian Explosion. However, although the process of microevolution has been demonstrated, Darwinian evolution is still a theory and fails to provide convincing evidence for the evolution of species and particularly of man (embodied with all of his amazing attributes) from a common ancestor of the ape. All of the data indicate that man is similar to other primates in morphology (size, shape, etc.) and DNA, but in other traits (emotional, intellectual and spiritual)

---

1. Several books have reported that the species that appeared during the Cambrian Explosion provided no evidence of ancestors; however, it is known that the Ediacara fauna preceded the Cambrian Explosion and that any previous soft-bodied species would not have been expected to survive to produce isolatable fossils.

man is entirely different and his origin is unexplainable except, as we shall see later, the result of a separate and unique event.

The author asks that the reader keep an open mind when reading this book and not cleave to preconceived notions that have their origin in highly charged emotional, but not necessarily factually based, positions.

Introduction

I can see how it might be possible for a man to look down upon the earth and be an atheist, but I cannot conceive how he could look into the heavens and say that there is no God.

Abraham Lincoln

EVERY DECADE IN THE TWENTIETH CENTURY HAS BEEN defined by an overwhelming question. In the 1970s the question was, What are we doing in Vietnam and how can we get out with honor? In the 1980s the question was, Is every person in the world entitled to inalienable human rights? In the 1990s the question was, How important are ethics and morality in business and in government? Today, at the beginning of the new millennium, this writer believes that the question for this decade will turn out to be, Is there really a God and, if so, who is he and what does he expect from us?

If one wants to know if there is a God, it would be important to address the questions of the origin of the universe and the origin of life. Namely, if there is a God, what is the evidence for his existence, what has he done and how has he acted in the past? These questions can only be answered if one can know whether the universe and life are the result of creative acts by God (or a "super intellect" as suggested by Einstein and Hawking) or are they the result of chance? It appears that many, if not most, scientists are reluctant to believe in creation because they believe that creation does not have a scientific basis, but is only a belief based strictly on faith.

Scientific beliefs based on religious faith have no place in science, and for good reason. When Copernicus (1473–1543) stated that the earth revolved around the sun and not the sun around the earth, the Catholic church became very unhappy because it believed (erroneously) that Copernicus' position was contrary to the Bible. Later, Galileo (1564–1642) provided further evidence to support the position of Copernicus; however, in 1633 he was called to Rome to stand trial for his published treatise, *Dialogo dei Massimi Sistemi*. He was found guilty of having "held and taught" Copernican doctrine and was subjected to house arrest until he died in 1642. The Catholic church has recently recognized its own error and has apologized for its actions against Galileo.

The church also has been involved in other important cases involving science and has made pronouncements in areas in which it was clearly not qualified to render an opinion. Further complications have arisen as a result of religious groups trying to convince science to conclude what they believe (erroneously) the Bible teaches. Since there should be no contradiction between what science and the Bible teaches, one must consider that when such a contradiction is assumed, it is a result of incorrect interpretation of one or the other. Herein lies one of the sources of confusion in the creation/evolution debate; some people are misinterpreting the Bible and other people are misinterpreting scientific data.

In the ensuing discussions it will become clear that creation does indeed have a scientific basis. This basis began to be established in the twentieth century, starting with the contributions of Einstein (1916) and Hubble (1929), and ending with data obtained from the COBE (Cosmic Background Explorer) satellite, which has provided cosmic background microwave radiation data (1990–1993) to support the big bang theory. If indeed the big bang theory is correct, then the universe had a beginning and hence it follows that it must have had an initiator of the beginning. Such was the conclusion of both Albert Einstein and Stephen Hawking who referred to the initiator of the beginning as a super intellect.

The subject of creation/evolution is a highly controversial topic. The overlying question is, can we treat the subject of creation/evolution in a purely intellectual manner or must this subject continue to be part of the cultural war between those who believe in God and those who don't, regardless of the truth and scientific observations? Among the top scientists in this country, members of the National Academy of Sciences, 90 percent profess to be either atheistic or agnostic (Larson and Witham, *Scientific American*, p. 90, September 1999). Philip E. Johnson has been instrumental in providing information from a creationist's perspective that indicates that the position presented to the public concerning the subject of creation/evolution has been a one-sided presentation in favor of evolution with overtones of "political correctness." He reports that the position of educators with respect to the subject of creation/evolution is exemplified by the position taken in the high school biology textbook by Neil A. Campbell, (*Biology*, 2nd ed., p. 434, 1990), that states, "Today nearly all biologists acknowledge that evolution is a fact. The term theory is no longer appropriate except when referring to the various models that attempt to explain how life evolved." This position of educators is supported by the National Education Association (NEA) which has taken the position that the theory of creation should not be discussed in the classrooms when discussing the theory of evolution. So much for freedom of speech and First Amendment rights!

After discussing the subject of alternative explanations for evolution, such as creation, with some of the top high school biology teachers in the state of Georgia, it became clear that the position for the origin of life as proceeding through an evolutionary process is considered "politically correct" and the alternative position for creation is not to be tolerated in the classroom. There is no valid scientific basis for this position as will become clear in this presentation.

One of the major problems that has caused such a polarization in the creation/evolution debate is the confusion that has come about due to the position of a group of Christians who call themselves "scientific creationists." These people hold that the earth is 6,000-10,000 years old, and was created in six 24-hour days as implied in the Bible, chapter 1 of the book of Genesis. Their position has gained wide acceptance. As will be pointed out later, the scientific evidence is clear that the universe is approximately 17 billion years old, the earth is approximately 4 billion years old and creation took place in six periods of time possibly millions of years apart. These scientific data do not refute the Bible, but are consistent with the Bible when one considers that the Hebrew word "yom" can mean not only a 24-hour day, but also can be interpreted as an epoch or a period of time.

The scientific creationist position has been supported mainly by ICR (Institute of Creation Research) in spite of overwhelming evidence to the contrary. The weakness of their position has attracted the ire of many scientists. An important point is that the position of scientific creationists should not be confused with the position of many scientists and laypeople who are Christians, call themselves creationists and who hold to the Bible as the inspired Word of God, yet accept the scientific evidence that the earth is 4 billion years old. It is the opinion of this writer that scientific creationists, although well meaning, have hurt the credibility of Christians to bring some understanding and unity to the creation/evolution controversy by maintaining completely indefensible positions.

The following quotes show just how polarized the creationist/evolutionist camps have become:

Quotes In Support of Evolution:

1. "I believe creationism is wrong, utterly and absolutely wrong. I would go further. There are degrees of being wrong. The creationists are at the bottom of the scale. What we must do—and here I speak to scientists, humanists and educators—is show scientific creationism for the wicked, sterile fraud it is." (M. Ruse, *New Scientist* 4, pp. 317-319, February 1982).

2. Richard Dawkins refers to creationists as "a gang of ignorant crackpots." (Richard Dawkins, "Against Alternative History," *Times*, Literary Supplement, November 1983).

3. Carl Sagan wrote that most Americans continue to believe that they were created by God despite everything that he and other prominent scientists have done to persuade them that nature is all there is. (Carl Sagan, *The Demon-Haunted World*, Random House, New York, 1996).

4. "In the evolutionary pattern of thought there is no longer either need or room for the supernatural. The earth was not created, it evolved. So did all the animals and plants that inhabit it, including our human selves, mind and soul as well as brain and body. So did religion." (Julian Huxley, Darwin Centennial Celebration at the University of Chicago, 1959.)

5. "Darwinism's theory is now supported by all available relevant evidence, and its truth is not doubted by any serious modern biologists." (Richard Dawkins, "The Necessity of Darwinism," *New Scientist* 15, p. 130, April 1982).

The latter comment by Dawkins is interesting considering that there are at least three Nobel Laureates (comments to follow) who disagree with his position.

The following quotes show clearly that the theory of Darwinian evolution is still considered by some competent scientists to be a theory, and not a fact:

Quotes in Support of Creation:

1. "There is a pretty widespread sense of dissatisfaction about what has come to be thought of as the accepted evolutionary theory in the English-speaking world, the so-called neo–Darwinian theory." (Sir Peter Medawar, Nobel Prize winner in physiology, Philadelphia, PA. Symposium, 1966.)

2. "An honest man, armed with all the knowledge available to us now, could only state that in some sense, the origin of life appears at the moment to be almost a miracle, so many are the conditions which would have had to have been satisfied to get it going." (Francis Crick, Nobel Prize winner in physiology, *Life Itself*, p. 88 Simon and Schuster, New York).

3. "The probability that at ordinary temperatures a macroscopic number of molecules is assembled to give rise to the highly ordered structures and to the coordination functions characterizing living organisms is vanishingly small. The idea of spontaneous genesis of life in its present form is therefore highly improbable even on the scale of the billions of years during which prebiotic evolution occurred." (Ilya Prigogine, Nobel Prize winner in chemistry, G. Nicolis and A. Babloyantz, *Physics Today*, p. 23-31, November 1972).

4. "To suppose that the eye with all its inimitable contrivances for adjusting the focus to different distances, for admitting different amounts of light, and for the correction of spherical and chromatic aberration, could have been formed by natural selection seems, I freely confess, absurd in the highest degree." (Charles Darwin, *The Origin of Species*, p. 168, 1859).

5. "There are no detailed Darwinian accounts for the evolution of any fundamental biochemical or cellular systems,

only a variety of wishful speculations. It is remarkable that Darwinism is accepted as a satisfactory explanation for such a vast subject—evolution—with so little rigorous examination of how well its basic theses work in illuminating specific instances of biological adaptation or diversity." (James Shapiro, University of Chicago, in the National Review of Michael Behe's book, *Darwin's Black Box,* 1998).

One of the most important problems that has caused polarization between creationists and evolutionists has been the inadequate definition of terms whenever the subject of creation/evolution is discussed. Just as a distinction should be made between the terms "creationist" and "scientific creationist," a distinction should also be made between the terms "evolutionist" and "Darwinian evolutionist." Evolution is defined as random mutation (or a copying error in DNA replication), followed by natural selection. Microevolution refers to a process of gradual change, usually within a species. Such evolution is well established and accepted by almost everyone. On the other hand, Darwinian evolution (macroevolution) refers to a process of gradual change that began with the first formed cell which in time has led to the formation of all species known today. This writer considers himself to be a scientist who believes in creation (a creationist), but who is not a scientific creationist (6,000-10,000 year old earth and six-day creation period), and who believes in the process of evolution (gradual change from one species to another) but not in Darwinian evolution in its broadest sense which relates all species back to the same single cell. When evolutionists use the term "evolution," they are generally referring to Darwinian evolution and when they use the term "creation," they are referring to scientific creationism. If everyone would pay more attention to these definitions, at least some of the problems in the area of creation/evolution would disappear.

We will see later in this discussion that the origin of man still lacks evidence for a definitive conclusion. However, the origin of man is not nearly as important a question as the origin of life which can be known with more certainty. Therefore, if the origin of life can be established as an act of intelligent design (creation by God?), then the origin of man almost becomes a moot point, at least until more information is available.

It is not surprising that in the beginning of the twenty-first century, the origin of man cannot be known with certainty. One century earlier (the beginning of the twentieth century), molecular biology, which is essential to the understanding of the origin of life, was essentially unknown. It is reasonable to believe that, one or two centuries from now, much more will be known concerning the molecular biology of hominids such that one will be able to speak in more definitive terms with respect to the origin of man. Nevertheless, a rational explanation for the origin of man will be presented that is consistent with both modern anthropology and the Bible.

I. The Origin of the Universe

It is difficult to discuss the beginning of the universe without mentioning the concept of God. My work on the origin of the universe is on the borderline between science and religion. But I try to stay this side of the border. It is quite possible that God acts in ways that cannot be described by Scientific laws.

Stephen Hawking in an interview with Hugh Downs,
20/20, July 21, 1989. Taken from Peter Bocchino,
Macro-Evolution: A Critic of First Principles.

A. The Age of the Universe and the Age of the Earth

THE UNIVERSE IS SO INCREDIBLY LARGE AND COMPLEX THAT to think about how it originated solely from energy is a concept difficult to even imagine, much less understand. Fortunately, due to the contributions of some brilliant astronomers and astrophysicists, considerable light has been shed on just how the universe came into existence.

The Bible says that the universe had a beginning; however 2,300 years ago Aristotle said that the universe is eternal. More recently, James Usher, Archbishop of Armagh in Ireland, said, based on biblical evaluation, that the universe began at 12:00 o'clock noon on October 23, 4004, BC. It is clear that early speculation as to the age of the universe by those without a scientific background has only caused confusion.

In more modern times, the position of scientific creationists has also confused one's understanding of the origin and age of the universe; however, Hugh Ross and others have worked diligently to remove the confusion. For example, Ross has reported that at least six different scientific methods have been used to determine the age of the universe (Table 1). All methods are in general agreement and show the universe to be approximately 17 billion years old.

Table 1.

Methods Used to Determine the Age of the Universe

Method	Billions of Years		
Globular cluster fitting	17.0	±	2.4
Nucleochronology	17.0	±	4.0
Hubble time	14.5	±	5.0
Expansion of the universe	14.5	±	5.0
Color—luminosity fitting	17.0	±	2.4
Anthropic principle	17	±	7

Adapted from Hugh Ross, *The Fingerprint of God*, Whitaker House, pp. 93, 159 (1989). Reprinted by permission of Whitaker House, New Kensington, PA.

According to studies in nucleochronology, evidence in favor of the age of the "old earth" (approximately 4 billion years) over the age of the "young earth" (6,000-10,000 years) lies mainly in determining the age of rocks, and fossils of plants, animals and human life by various dating techniques. The main technique involves radioactive isotope dating. This method is based on the fact that some elements are radioactive (i.e., disintegrate at a constant rate, at atmospheric temperature and pressure to produce alpha or beta particles, or gamma rays) and decay in a known fashion to produce stable elements. The half-life of an element is the time required for one half of all of the atoms of that element to decay to its daughter product(s).

Equation 1 shows the decay of uranium-238 to thorium-234 and helium-4 (an alpha particle).

$$^{238}\text{U} \quad \rightarrow \quad ^{234}\text{Th} + {}^{4}\text{He} \qquad\qquad (\text{eq.1})$$

Table 2 lists several radioactive elements and their half lives.

Table 2.

Half lives (t$^{1/2}$) of some Radioactive Elements

Element	t$^{1/2}$
^{80}Br	17.6 minutes
^{28}Mg	21 hours
^{234}Th	24.1 days
^{14}C	5,730 years
^{235}U	713 million years
^{40}K	1.3 billion years
^{238}U	4.5 billion years

The fact that certain radioactive elements like ^{238}U with a half life of 4.5 billion years are still found today in the earth's crust shows that the earth cannot be significantly more than 4.5 billion years old. The fact that other radioactive elements like ^{14}C, which can be prepared in the laboratory and its half life determined independently (5,730 years) no longer exist today shows that this element has completely decayed to its non-radioactive daughter product (eq. 2) and therefore the age

$$^{14}C \quad \rightarrow \quad ^{14}N \ + \ e^- \qquad\qquad \text{(eq. 2)}$$

of the earth must be greater than the $t^{\frac{1}{2}}$ value of this element. Actually, a radioactive element can be detected after at least ten times the $t^{\frac{1}{2}}$ value since the $t^{\frac{1}{2}}$ value represents decay of only one half of all of the atoms. Therefore ^{14}C could be detected after at least 57,300 years (ten half lives) if not longer. The fact that ^{14}C cannot be detected in any carbon compounds today that are taken from nonliving sources shows that the earth cannot be 6,000-10,000 years old, but must be older than 57,300 years. Other methods involving the radioactive dating of rocks involves the determination of relative amounts of radioactive elements found in a rock sample with respect to its degradation products, e.g.,

$$^{40}K/^{40}Ar \ , \quad ^{87}Rb/^{87}Sr, \quad ^{232}Th/^{206}Pb$$

Scientific creationists attempt to discard the validity of radioactive isotope dating in order to hold to a 6,000-10,000 year old earth. They have provided no compelling arguments to overcome the validity of radioisotope dating which has been clearly supported by numerous scientific methods. If indeed the scientific creationists are correct about 24-hour day creation periods, then land animals and man were created during the same 24-hour period (the sixth day of creation). However, it is well established through the fossil record that land animals appeared millions of years before man.

B. The Big Bang Theory of the Origin of the Universe

Several models have been suggested to describe the origin and present status of the universe, including a steady state model, an oscillating model and an infinite hesitation model. The one model that appears to be accepted by most modern cosmologists is the big bang model. The big bang theory was initially proposed by George Gamow in 1946 and further supported by Penzias and Wilson of Bell Telephone Laboratories by analysis of cosmic background microwave radiation data. Penzias and Wilson were awarded the Nobel Prize in 1978 for their contributions.

The big bang theory suggests that the universe began when a volume of energy less than the size of a pinhead, at nearly infinite temperature, pressure and density, exploded. This explosion converted energy into mass according to Einstein's equation (eq. 3).

$$E = MC^2 \qquad\qquad\qquad \text{(eq. 3)}$$

Where:
E = energy,
M = mass,
C = velocity of light (186,000 miles/sec.)

The result of the explosion is still taking place and the universe is both expanding and decelerating (recent unconfirmed reports suggest that the expansion of the universe is accelerating) at a rate expected for an explosion. Initially only hydrogen was formed; however, at 5 million degrees, fusion of hydrogen to helium takes place. This fusion of hydrogen to helium is what is taking place in stars. The hydrogen content in stars is approximately 90 percent and the helium content is approximately 9 percent with all of the other elements formed accounting for the remaining 1 percent. At the core of the star where the temperature is the hottest (30 to 100 million degrees) fusion to higher elements, up to iron (Fe) in the periodic chart, takes place. Elements higher than iron in the periodic chart are formed only during a supernova when temperatures as high as 400 million degrees are reached. Hugh Ross suggests that stars began to form approximately 2 billion years after the initial big bang explosion. Because a star is burning hydrogen to produce energy in the form of heat and light, the time will come when there is insufficient hydrogen remaining to sustain the star and it will go through a dying process. The star will eventually explode with incredible force spewing out into the universe all of the heavier elements produced in its inner core. This explosion is called a "nova" and explosion of a large star is called a "supernova." It is estimated that a supernova produces the light of 100 billion stars. Ross suggests that novae started to happen 10-12 billion years after the universe began. It is believed that the higher elements, when released by exploding stars, then agglomerate in the universe over a long period of time to form the planets (asteroids, etc.) known today. It is estimated that approximately 100 tons of celestial dust falls on the earth each day.

The incredible results obtained by the COBE satellite (1990–1993) are considered the best evidence for the big bang theory of the origin of the universe. The resulting cosmic background microwave radiation data when evaluated is perfectly consistent with that expected for an explosion. Temperature data from the COBE satellite are consistent with the initial temperature of the explosion being very high and the present temperature of the universe being very low (observed to be -270° F) because of the cooling effect experienced as a result of an expanding universe. Stephen Hawking called the results of the COBE satellite "the discovery of the century, if not of all time" and "what we have found is evidence for the birth of the universe." Hawking concluded from the

COBE satellite data that since the universe had a beginning then there must have been an initiator of the beginning which he referred to as a "super intellect." Hawking does not accept the concept of a personal God; however, accepting that the universe had a beginning which was initiated by a super intellect can be interpreted as an indirect endorsement of creation proposed by one of the leading scientists of all time. Indeed the results of the COBE satellite are considered by many to have both scientific and theological implications. In addition, the results obtained from the Hubble telescope have been of tremendous value, for these findings have allowed the observation of galaxies near the limit of the universe. Edwin Hubble has also been able to measure the distance between galaxies and the rates at which they are moving away from each other. All Hubble findings support the big bang theory.

Further evidence for the big bang theory comes from Einstein's work represented by his theory of general relativity. Einstein's theory is expressed by equation 4 which is a mathematical statement that relates time, space, matter and motion of the universe. The term on the left side of the equation is an acceleration term and on the right are known constants.

$$2 \; \frac{d^2 R}{R \, dt^2} \; = \; \frac{8\pi G}{3} \left(\rho + \frac{3P}{C^2} \right) \qquad \text{(eq. 4)}$$

Where:
R = Scale factor for the universe
t = Time
k = Constant describing the geometry of the universe
C = Speed of light
G = Constant of gravity
P = Total pressure arising from all sources
ρ = Density of matter and radiation

There are several different tests of Einstein's theory of general relativity. For example, in 1919 Eddington showed that starlight was bent by the sun's gravitational field by 1.778° - 1.802° (° = arc seconds); Einstein's equation predicts 1.751°. Einstein's equation provides the determination of the moment of explosion and evidence for a ten dimensional space and time creation model exhibited in the first 10^{-43} seconds of the big bang. Calculations show that matter and energy can be traced back to the beginning of the universe, and since matter and energy had a beginning, Einstein concluded that there must be an initiator of the beginning. Like Hawking, Einstein did not believe in a personal God, but he did believe that some force was responsible for initiating the universe. Since man has only four dimensions of space and time, it is interesting to consider that six additional dimensions necessitated in the creation process must also be exhibited by the initiator of the creation process. Only future scientific advances will be able to specify the nature of these other dimensions. What an incredible time that will be!

C. The Anthropic Principle

It has been suggested that if the energy of the big bang was different by one part in 10^{120} parts, there would be no life anywhere in the universe (S.W. Einberg, "Life in the Universe," *Scientific American*, October 1994). Such a statement can be supported by what is known today as the "anthropic principle" which was first introduced by the cosmologist Brandon Carter in 1974. The anthropic principle was expounded upon further in a series of books by Paul Davies (Templeton Prize, 1995), a volume on the anthropic principle was written by Frank J. Tipler and John D. Barrow and later the anthropic principle was further defined and popularized by Hugh Ross. The Anthropic Principle states that the universe possesses unique and narrowly defined characteristics essential to the support of life on earth. Ross in his book, *The Creator and the Cosmos*, and subsequent books, provides more than 50 examples of the anthropic principle. For example, life on earth could not exist if the earth had a slower or faster rotation, if the earth was smaller or larger, if the moon was smaller or larger, the oxygen/nitrogen ratio was smaller or larger, etc.

It is interesting that Michael Denton (*Nature's Destiny—How the Laws of Biology Reveal Purpose in the Universe*, Free Press, 1998) demonstrates a biological anthropic principle showing that the laws of nature are uniquely suited for the existence of the carbon-based life that exists on earth. Some of Denton's examples show the uniqueness of the properties of water (density, freezing point, boiling point, hydrogen bonding properties) that are essential to the life of a cell, the life cycle of plants, animals, etc., the uniqueness of carbon as the backbone of most compounds of biological significance, the uniqueness of carbon dioxide as a buffer for biological systems, etc. Thus life on earth would not exist if it were not for some very unique and specific properties of water, carbon, buffers, and so on.

The question, of course is, Is it a coincidence that planet earth possesses all of these narrowly defined criteria to support life, or have all of these criteria been purposely designed into the universe by a super intellect in order to make life possible? Probability calculations indicate that it is highly unlikely, but not impossible, that the exact conditions on planet earth are duplicated anywhere else in the universe.

Considerable effort has been expended by astronomers to obtain evidence for life in the universe outside of planet earth. Toward this end, reportedly 2 billion dollars have been spent in the past 20 years by the U.S. government in sponsored research. The SETI (Search for Extra Terrestrial Intelligence) program, using radio telescopes and giant receivers designed to detect any kind of response to signals that have been sent into space, so far has not been successful. Initial efforts with project OZMA involved listening to two nearby stars for radio signals. Later much more sophisticated efforts were made involving project SERENDIP and project Phoenix which are still in operation. It is interesting that if only one signal from space was received, it would be interpreted as a sign of extra-terrestrial intelligence. However, when thousands of signs are received with respect to the exact chemistry exhibited by the human body, intelligent design is not accepted as an explanation for the observations.

It has been suggested by Hoyle et al (*Evolution from Space*, 1981, Dent and Sons, London) and others that life on earth was seeded by chemicals from outer space. This phenomenon is called "panspermia." Analysis of a large well-known meteorite in Murcheson, Australia, showed a number of compounds, such as benzene, naphthalene, biphenyl, etc., all of which fall in the categories of hydrocarbons and polynuclear hydrocarbons. There were also indications of small amounts of some amino acids, but not carbohydrates and lipids; those compounds needed to form a cell. There is a big difference between a few chemicals and a living organism. Absolutely no evidence exists that life on earth was seeded by chemicals from outer space.

D. The Magnitude of the Universe

Only an astronomer or astrophysicist could have a broad understanding and appreciation of the universe; however, recent pictures obtained from the Hubble telescope are exquisite to the point of humbling any viewer. If one observes picture after picture of the universe, one becomes mesmerized, if not stunned, at the exotic beauty and perceived complex chemistry and physics of the nebulae and galaxies observed, and the enormity of the dimensions involved. The universe is 5 billion light years (2.93×10^{22} miles) in radius. There are over 200 billion stars in our galaxy (the Milky Way galaxy) and there are over 200 billion galaxies. The Milky Way galaxy is 70,000 light years (which is 4.11 x 10^{17} miles or 411,000,000,000,000,000 miles) in diameter. In order to indicate the enormity of this number (4.11 x 10^{17}), one would have to travel at the rate of 100 miles per second for 130 million years in order to travel from one end of the Milky Way galaxy to the other. The largest nebula (star and planet forming area of celestial gas and dust) in the Milky Way galaxy is the Eta Carinae nebula (Figure 1) which is 200 light years wide (1.17 x 10^{15} miles) and is 9,000 light years (5.27 x 10^{16} miles) from planet earth. Traveling at 100 miles per second, it would take 17 million years to travel from planet earth to the Eta Carinae nebula.

The numbers of stars, planets and galaxies, and the distances involved in their separation, speak to an incredibly vast universe in which planet earth is no more conspicuous than a grain of sand on the beach. Yet there is no evidence that there is another planet exactly like it. If evolution can explain the appearance of life on planet earth, then evolution would be expected to produce living species on other planets in the universe considering the large number of other planets that exist. Of course, we do not know with certainty that there is not another planet in the universe with exactly the same properties of planet earth and, if such a planet exists, we do not know if beings such as man exist on that planet. Also, we do not know if there exists another planet, differing in the characteristics of planet earth, which might contain some form of life unlike anything present on planet earth. There are at least 50 other stars in the Milky Way galaxy that are associated with planets. The question as to the existence of extraterrestrial intelligence in the universe has both scientific and theological implications and cannot be answered with any certainty at this time. What kind of super intellect could have created such an incredibly enormous, yet deftly precise, universe?

Figure 1.
The Eta Carinae NEBULA
This nebula is composed of a mixture of gases and dust and is the
largest known star-forming nebula in the Milky Way galaxy.

(Photograph by Bob Sandness, in Astronomy 1989, edited by Terence Dickinson,
1998, Firefly Books Ltd.). Reproduced by permission of Bob Sandness. This picture is shown in color on the book cover.

E. Conclusions Concerning the Origin of the Universe

Scientific evidence for the creation model of the universe is both clear and overwhelming. Contributions by Einstein and Hawking, and data from the Hubble telescope and the COBE satellite, provide convincing evidence for the big bang theory and the age of the universe (~17 billion years). The big bang theory supports the premise that the universe had a beginning and therefore needed an originator of the beginning. The universe has continued to evolve (change) from the time of the big bang from a small volume of energy to the present time involving an incredibly large universe. Convincing evidence involving radioactive isotope dating establishes the age of the earth to be approximately 4 billion years. Although there is no evidence of extraterrestrial intelligence, the possibility of some kind of life outside of planet earth cannot be excluded. None of these conclusions violate the integrity of the Bible (book of Genesis, chapter 1) that says God initiated the beginning of the universe. Students entering the university armed with the known scientific facts about the origin of the universe should not be put into an embarrassing and untenable position of trying to defend a 6,000-10,000 year old earth as a part of their religious faith.

Some of the problems in the creation/evolution controversy have been caused by scientific creationists who have interpreted the book of Genesis on the grounds of strict and uncompromising scientific and historical analysis. From the time of Moses, who is believed to have written the book of Genesis, to the present time, Christians believe that the Bible is both historically and scientifically accurate. The Dead Sea Scrolls support this position. However, before the time of Moses, the historical and scientific interpretation of the creation event is more complicated because, for example, no human being was present during that event. Therefore, Moses could not have known firsthand about the specific details of creation except by revelation from God Himself. It is suggested that the details of creation given by God to Moses presented in the book of Genesis, chapter 1, were presented in a way that was in keeping with the level of Moses' understanding of the universe at that time in history. Since Moses was in no intellectual position at the time to understand and write in a quantitative sense what actually happened, it is not surprising that the creation event was not described in terms of explosion radiation phenomena, planet trajectories, galaxy interactions, black holes and chemical composition of the atmosphere, but rather in events from the creation of the heavens to the creation of man in a language Moses could understand.

The complexity and magnificence of the universe—expressed by mathematicians, astrophysicists and astronomers—attests to an incredibly powerful and intelligent force or person who could produce such a result. If this force is God, it is not surprising that he would create a universe that would continue to reveal his magnificence over a long period of time and keep mankind in a state of awe as the mysteries of his creation are uncovered.

II. The Origin of Man

Among the scenes which are deeply impressed on my mind, none exceed in sublimity the primeval forest undefaced by the hand of man; whether those of Brazil, where the powers of Life are predominant, or those of Tierra del Fuego, where Death and Decay prevail. Both are temples filled with the varied productions of the God of Nature—no one can stand in these solitudes unmoved, and not feel that there is more in man than the mere breath of his body.

Excerpt from the journal of Charles Darwin's voyage,
1831–1836, written in 1837.
Charles Darwin, *The Voyage of the H.M.S.,
Beagle,* Heritage Press, p. 459. (1957).

A. Introduction

THE VASTNESS, COMPLEXITY, BEAUTY AND ORDER OF THE universe is indeed breathtaking; however, all of these adjectives and more can be used to describe the biochemistry, molecular biology and physiology of life. It is only in the last 30 years that our understanding of many biological processes relating to plant, animal and human life has become much clearer. The most recent success in determining the exact composition of the human genome attests to the incredible progress in biochemistry and molecular biology. To those who have some background in biochemistry and molecular biology, a description of many detailed biological processes is like watching the *Swan Lake* ballet or listening to Rimsky-Korsakov's *Scheherazade*. Both exhibit incredible preciseness and beauty, and inspire one to contemplate who could be the originator of such things.

B. History of the Evolutionary Concept of Life

Although societies from the beginning of time have consisted of some percentage of pagans, atheists, agnostics, hedonists, naturalists, secular humanists, and so on, many people since the time of Moses believed in the God of the Bible and believed that he was the creator of the universe and life. It wasn't until 1859 when Charles Darwin published his book, *The Origin of Species*, that the major belief of many people that God was the creator of the universe and life was challenged. Darwin's position after 20 years of research was that man is the result of evolution from a previous species, and that all species can be traced back to previous species from which they evolved. By the standards of 1859, Darwin's work represented a scholarly evaluation of the possible evolution of many species by comparing mainly the morphology (bone structure, height, cranium size, kinds of teeth, etc.) of the fossil remains of one species with respect to another. Darwin's comparison of a number of species, such as finches in the Gallapagos Islands, showed that the beak size and plumage of such finches changed over a period of time by adaptation to changes in environment. This is an example of microevolution (change of one species to another species of similar morphology). There are many examples of microevolution and no serious scientist would argue to the contrary. Figure 2 shows the microevolution of the horse from the species Eohippus (60 million years ago) to the species Equus which is the present-day horse. Although there are some morphological changes over a long period of time, it is clear that such changes are to be expected due to changes in diet and the environment. Clearly this evolutionary process does not represent the change of one *kind* of species to an entirely different *kind* of species as one would interpret the word "kind" used in the Bible. However, Darwinian theory does propose that a species of one kind can evolve to a species of an entirely different kind; a species that is quite different in morphology, e.g., the evolution of a bird from a dinosaur (archaeoraptor).

Darwin's theory of evolution (gradualism) suggests that the change of one species to another (random gene mutation followed by natural selection) takes place gradually over a long period of time (possibly millions of years) and that all species originated from the same single cell. Such a process should involve the formation of many intermediate species in proceeding from one species to another. For example, since Homo

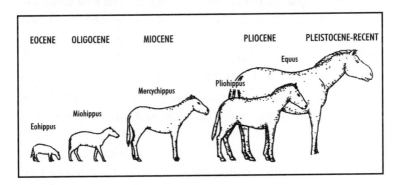

Figure 2.
The Evolution of the Horse from Eohippus to Equus, an Example of Microevolution.

(Adapted from Storer, Usinger, Nybakken and Stebbins, *Elements of Zoology*, 4th ed, McGraw-Hill, p. 212, 1977). Reproduced by permission of The McGraw-Hill Companies.

sapiens (man) are said to have evolved from a species common to the ape, then anthropologists should have unearthed many intermediary species (missing links) to establish this connection similar to the case of the horse just mentioned. Darwin has stated in his book, *The Origin of Species* (p. 191), that if such intermediate species are not found in the future, then his theory would collapse. The fact is that evolutionists have claimed that several intermediate species have been found, e.g., australopithecus, bosei, homo erectus, Neanderthal man, etc., relating man to a common ancestor of the ape; however, every so-called "missing link" has been classified as an ape. Even though the above species may be related to man, it is not clear that the relationship is the result of a Darwinian evolutionary process. On the other hand, creationists maintain that more definitive species relating man to a common ancestor of the ape (missing links) are still missing.

In addition to Darwin's book, there are two other much less substantive, but nonetheless significant, contributions to the early acceptance of evolutionary theory. The first contribution was the result of the Wilberforce–Huxley debate (1860), concerning the plausibility of the theory of evolution. Wilberforce was the bishop of Oxford and Huxley was a biologist. Wilberforce had no scientific training and was easy prey for the forceful and dynamic Huxley. The victory of Huxley over Wilberforce was overwhelming and considered further proof of the theory of evolution.

Another debate took place in 1925 which has been referred to in history as the "Scopes Monkey Trial." This debate took place between William Jennings Bryan (three-time presidential candidate and noted fundamentalist and Christian) and Clarence Darrow (a popular defense attorney). The debate was highly publicized and was a setup by the ACLU who wisely picked the two combatants and the case. The teacher on trial for teaching evolution was not the biology teacher, but rather an athletic coach who was substituting in the biology class for two weeks. Bryan was no match for Darrow and was humiliated during the trial due to his ineptness. Unfortunately, Darrow's victory was perceived as a victory for the theory of evolution, although neither debater was qualified to debate the real scientific issues of evolution. The trial was later made into a movie (*Inherit the Wind*) in which Bryan and his supporters were portrayed as fundamentalist bigots and Darrow was portrayed as the hero. Such is the impression that Hollywood and the media provided in order to support their own beliefs.

Nevertheless from 1925 to the present day, the teaching of evolution in ninth grade biology throughout the country is considered the accepted theory of the origin of man, and the discussion of creation as an alternative theory is forbidden in the classroom. It is the opinion of this writer that the teaching of scientific creationism, with its lack of scientific merit, has brought us to this point and has eliminated the possibility of openly debating the theory of creation in the classroom. On the other hand, it will become obvious later in this discussion that Darwinian evolution does not satisfactorily explain the origin of man in all of his uniqueness and particularly does not explain the origin of life.

Additional cases of error or outright fraud involving major debating points by evolutionists can be found in two reports. The first case involves a famous and often quoted report by Ernest Haeckel a century ago that shows the similarity of human and animal embryos. Haeckel compared the embryos at different stages of development and concluded that both the human and animal embryos had common evolutionary roots (Figure 3). This particular reference has been a classic in support of Darwinian evolution and can be found in many biology textbooks, even today, including the most prestigious book on the cell, Alberts et al, *Molecular Biology of the Cell*, 2nd ed.,

Garland Publishing Inc., p. 31 (1989). The *Washington Times* (national weekly edition), January 25-31, 1999, reported that British embryologist Michael Richardson visited Jena University in Germany to study Haeckel's work and concluded that Haeckel

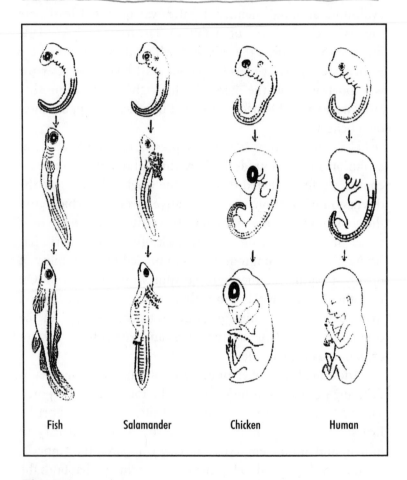

| Fish | Salamander | Chicken | Human |

Figure 3.
Embryo comparisons
Four different species shown to exhibit very similar stages in the early development of embryos.

(Adapted from E. Haeckel, *The Evolution of Man*, Engelmann, 1874).

"doctored" his drawings to make the embryos look identical. The Haeckel drawings have been used as a major argument by evolutionists such as Carl Sagan who held that abortion is justified because the vertebrate embryos of several species of animals have been shown to be identical to that of a human being. Jonathan Wells, a research biologist at the University of California at Berkeley, has taken a position that the difference in embryos contradicts Darwin's idea that all creatures descended from a common ancestor.

The second case involves an equally popular report by Bernard Kettlewell, an Oxford zoologist, describing an example of natural selection. Kettlewell proposed that black and white peppered moths adapt to urban pollution and that natural selection does occur in nature. Kettlewell observed that white moths were observed in the areas of light colored tree bark and dark colored moths were found in industrially polluted ones where the trees and rocks were darkened by pollution. It was proposed that the white and dark species survived in their particular areas because each was better camouflaged and therefore less visible toward their major predator, the bird. Steven J. Gould, world famous paleontologist, used the peppered moth as one of two examples to support the principle of natural selection discussed in his classic book *Science and Creationism*, Oxford University Press, p. 121 (1984). More recently, however, a report by Theodore Sargent, a biologist at the University of Massachusetts, has shown that peppered moths change color under many conditions and do not actually live on tree trunks. Jerry Coyne, a biologist at the University of Chicago, reported in the journal *Nature* that the peppered moth example was "the prize horse in our stable" to illustrate evolution by natural selection but now this example has to be thrown out. Actually, the peppered moth report is a very poor example to indicate evolution by natural selection since color change does not indicate speciation.

One should not get the impression that natural selection is not a valid process because there is overwhelming evidence that it is; however, these very popular examples, used early in textbooks, were fraudulent or incorrect, but nevertheless played a role in directing support for the theory of evolution. Valid examples of natural selection can be found in Mengel's work on wood warblers and the drosophila fruit fly which was shown to evolve at least 600 species of fruit fly as determined by sequential arrangements. The female fruit fly produces 200–300 progeny which are short lived and therefore billions of progeny can be produced over a relatively short period of time. These circumstances explain why the fruit fly is such a good choice for establishing the validity of natural selection. However, the drosophila fruit fly and the wood warblers evolved only closely related species of the same kind and not of a different kind (genus, family, etc.). Natural selection is really not an issue. What is an issue is not whether the fruit fly can evolve into another species of its kind, but if the fruit fly can evolve into an entirely different kind of species, e.g., a bird. Clearly, microevolution is to be expected and has been observed many times; the evidence for broad-based macroevolution (Darwinian evolution) is lacking. Philip E. Johnson said it well in his book *Defeating Darwinism*, "Evolution is not about how an elephant evolved from a mouse, but where did the mouse come from in the first place."

There has been a very strong effort on the part of anthropologists and paleontologists to establish the connection between man and other primates such as the chimpanzee and gorilla. In all fairness, there is enough evidence (morphology and DNA) to make the proposal appear reasonable. However, the case is far from "convincing" and is therefore argumentative. It would be very helpful in this discussion to keep an open mind. It is suggested that man's proposed appearance via an evolutionary process does not preclude a separate creation process based on biochemical relationships similar to other primates. In this process it can be proposed that God instilled in man an intellect, soul and spirit at the time of his appearance that made him in the image and likeness of God, unlike other primates. This is a possibility that should be considered.

C. Anthropology and Missing Links

The study of anthropology involves an attempt to reconstruct the course of human evolution by examining the fossil remains of ancient humanlike species. A fossil represents the preserved remains of an ancient species most often found in sedimentary rock, peat bogs, frigid regions, etc. Somewhere between 3 and 20 million species have been detected. A number of well-publicized species considered to be missing links relating man to the ape have been reported in the past; however, these reports have been shown to be either fraudulent or in error. The following examples are provided to establish this point.

Table 3.

Missing Links (?)

Archaeopteryx	The world's most primitive bird fossil first reported in 1861 with teeth and claws on wings, said to have evolved from a reptile. Several birds have teeth and some have claws on wings, e.g., the ostrich. Fifty percent of the biology of an organism resides in its soft anatomy. Birds differ greatly from reptiles with respect to the central nervous system and the cardiovascular and respiratory systems. The cranial endocast shows typical avian hemispheres and the

49

cerebellum of a bird. (Jerison, "Brain Evolution and Archaeopteryx," *Nature*. 219, pp. 1381-82, 1968).

Archaeoraptor	A bird with a birdlike body and dinosaur-like tail, discovered in Lisoning, China, was reported to have evolved from a dinosaur. It was reported in the year 2000 to have been glued together from fossils of a true bird and a theropod dinosaur.
Neanderthal man	DNA shows a separate species from man. Comparing 378 base pairs of the Neanderthal's mitochondrial DNA to that of modern humans, researchers found an average of 27 differences between modern man and Neanderthal DNA. These differences are far more than the typical variation of eight among modern humans.
Piltdown man	Shown to be a hoax. An ape jaw was attached to a human skull. The skull was 10,000 years older than the jawbone.
Java man	Discredited by the discoverer.
Peking man	Suggested because human bones were found with ape skulls. (People at that time ate ape and monkey brains.)
Nebraska man	Entire person envisioned from a single tooth, later shown to be a pig's tooth.
Lucy	An example of austrolopithecus afrensis. Reclassified as an ape.
Ramapithecus	A jaw and teeth dismissed as early human in origin (orangutan).

These examples are not given in an attempt to discredit the work of anthropologists and paleontologists who have worked very diligently to collect and evaluate fossil remains. Such an impression would be wrong since such scientists have contributed greatly to a better understanding of fossil origins. On the other hand, the so-called missing links just mentioned played a large role early in the shaping of public opinion in favor of Darwinian evolution when the cases presented were not valid.

In a recent television program (June 18, 2003) on the Discovery channel entitled "Walking with Cavemen," the definite conclusion by the viewing audience was that more than great poetic license had been used to humanize early primate species. Lucy, for example, was portrayed as a thinking, emotional mother of two offspring, led by a male 25 years old who later lost his life in a fight with a marauding ape. Lucy was shown to mourn the leader, showed how she drank water and how invaders hid in reed beds in an attempt to capture her. The detailed story had the flavor of a television "soap." What a shame that an attempt is still being made by the media to deceive the public with regard to the acceptance of evolution. Hopefully, in the future, a valid balanced scientific presentation can be made by the media which maintains scientific integrity. Deception only delays the establishment of the truth.

One can find in many places a discussion of the evolution of primates from the first hominids beginning with the australopithecines 4.5 million years ago, to the species homo habilis 1.8 million years ago, to the species homo erectus 1.0 million years ago, to the species homo Neanderthalensis 150,000 years ago. Evidence of intelligence for the above species as deduced from tool making of the simplest objects (stone pieces that could be used for cutting purposes) is weak and argumentative at best. One could very well list these species as the so-called missing links leading to man; however, DNA results show that these species belong to the category of apes. On the other hand, evidence of modern human intelligence as assessed by paintings, development of advanced tools, establishment of clothes and housing, etc. was determined to first appear about 100,000 years ago.

In the Cambrian Explosion 540 million years ago, thousands of marine species appeared suddenly. Charles Walcott, director of the Smithsonian Institute, reported in 1909–1917 the recovery of 80,000 species of worms, insects, fish, etc., from the Burgess Shale located high in the Canadian Rockies in Yoho National Park on the eastern border of British Columbia (Briggs, Erwin and Collier, *The Fossils of the Burgess Shale*, Smithsonian Institute Press, 1994). The fact that these species appeared simultaneously and abruptly argues against "gradualism" (Darwinian evolution) as the method to explain the evolution of life. In an attempt to explain the relatively sudden appearance of so many species, Stephen J. Gould (*New Scientist* 2, p. 374, 1979) introduced the theory of "punctuated equilibrium"[2] which holds that these species arose within a period of thousands of years and have stayed unchanged for millions of years. Seventy phyla appeared at the time of the Cambrian Explosion; 40 have since disappeared. This incredible discovery was further verified by Raymond in 1930, Whittington in 1960 and Gould in 1987. The Burgess Shale discovery represents a major argument against the validity of the theory of gradualism (Darwinian evolution). (Stephen J. Gould, *Wonderful Life. The Burgess Shale and the Nature of History*, W.W. Norton and Company, 1987).

Paleontological studies show that 250 million years ago, 95 percent of all marine life suffered a massive extinction (thought to have been due to a catastrophic volcanic eruption). It is also reported that a meteor impact 65 million years

---

2. Punctuated equilibrium has been defined as the sudden appearance of species followed by millions of years of genetic stability, further followed by brief periods of rapid changes.

ago, with the force of well over 100 trillion tons of TNT, killed all the dinosaurs. Why have dinosaurs not reappeared in the past 65 million years via an evolutionary process? The answer that conditions on the earth are now different does not seem to be convincing.

It has been reported recently that man began his appearance on earth 70-120 thousand years ago. This conclusion came about by analysis of data obtained by the DNA tracing of man originating in North Africa and then migrating to different parts of the world. If man had existed before that time, there should be a much broader based DNA pattern describing people today than there is. The much narrower DNA pattern observed today could also be ascribed to man being much older, but having been subjected to a massive extinction leaving only a few people (possibly related) to begin a narrowly defined DNA pattern. Once again it appears that man is a relatively recent species on the face of the earth, appearing long after other primate species such as the gorilla, chimpanzee and orangutan.

Anthropology is a most fascinating and important area of research; however, this area of science does not require rigorous substantiating evidence to prove a point as does chemistry or physics. The physical sciences would not allow publication of speculation or suggestions without significant evidence to substantiate the claims. Figure 4 shows bone fragments from the fossil skeleton AL 288-1, now known as "Lucy," which has resulted in speculation as to the: height, weight, sex, shape, environmental circumstances, diet and behavior surrounding the proposed species. How can one accurately draw conclusions, based on such bone fragments, that Lucy might be a missing link between man and a common ancestor of the ape? It is interesting that different investigators have drawn substantially different pictures of Lucy based on the same bone fragments. Further study has shown Lucy (3-1/2 feet tall, weight 60

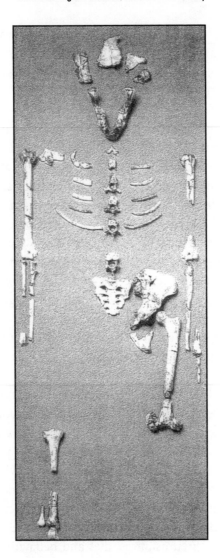

Figure 4.
"Lucy"- recovered bones.

(John Haywood, *The Illustrated History of Early Man*, Smithmark Publishing Co., p. 21, 1995.) Picture of recovered bones by John Reader, Science Photo Library/The Photo Library.) Reprinted by permission from Photo Researchers Inc.

pounds, brain 415cc) to be an example of australopithecus afarensis that is 3.5 million years old and not of human origin.

The following statement summarizes a general impression by many scientists that anthropological findings have not provided an answer to the questions surrounding the origin of man.

"The fossil record has provided none of the crucial transitional forms required by evolution. If such forms exist why do we not find them embedded in countless numbers in the crust of the earth?" (G.G. Simpson, a leading paleontologist, the Darwin Centenary Symposium, Chicago, Illinois, 1959).

One of the weaknesses of anthropology in its explanation of evolution is that anthropologists know little about biochemistry and molecular biology. Instead of realizing the significance of these areas, they ignore them. It can be shown that one cannot draw conclusions based primarily on morphology, but must look below the surface of the skin to determine the biochemistry and physiology of a species that are the major determinants in its evolutionary development. In an attempt to relate a species of one kind to a species of a different kind, it has not been possible to correlate the cardiovascular, respiratory, reproductive and central nervous systems in terms of Darwinian evolution. Unfortunately for paleontologists, only the hard parts of an organism fossilize, therefore not all organisms survive over a long period of time and thus are not available for further study.

Once again, it is suggested that part of the confusion in this area is due to the lack of distinction between the terms "evolution" and "Darwinian evolution." If evolution means gradual change over a long period of time in which one species of a kind forms a different species of the same kind or a similar kind, then most, if not all, people believe in evolution. However, as mentioned earlier, when evolutionists refer to evolution, they really mean Darwinian evolution which holds that all species have evolved from previous species and initially from the same single cell. Figures 5 and 6 are presented as simple examples of the problem of explaining Darwinian evolution by mutation followed by natural selection. For example, how many successful mutations followed by natural selection deep in the ocean would it take for both the humpback whale and the marine spider to have evolved from a common ancestor, especially considering the infrequency of mutations, the fact that the vast majority of mutations do not lead to viable organisms, none of the intermediate species have been observed, and the observations that the marine spider lives deep in the ocean by heat vents whereas the humpback whale thrives best in arctic waters.

Figure 5.
Colossendeis Colossae, a Deep-water Marine Spider.
This spider is found along the ocean floor by heat vents.

Sketch by Linda McMorris of Atlanta, GA.

The following quote by Michael Denton (*Evolution: A Theory in* Crisis, 1986, Adler and Adler) is instructive:

There is no doubt that as far as his macroevolutionary claims were concerned Darwin's central problem in the origin lay in the fact that he had absolutely no direct emperical evidence for the existence of clearcut intermediates that evolution on a major scale had ever occurred and that any of the major divisions of nature had been crossed gradually through a sequence of transitional forms. Over and over, he returns to the same problem, confessing that: 'the distinctness of specific forms and their not being blended together by innumerable transitional links is a very obvious difficulty'" (Charles Darwin, *The Origin of Species*, 6th ed. 1962, Collier Books).

Figure 6.
A Humpback Whale
This whale is ~60 ft long and travels mainly in frigid waters off the Antarctic continent.

Sketch by Linda McMorris of Atlanta, GA.

The major emphasis in the distinction between man and a previous primate species lies in those considerations that show man to be very different from other primate species such as the gorilla, orangutan or chimpanzee. Such primates have shown little sign of intellectual advancement in the past 65 million years, whereas man has shown incredible intellectual advancement in the past 200 years. At one time it was believed that the difference in intellect between man and the ape was due to brain size. More recently, excavations of primate skulls have been shown to exhibit cranium cavities not much different than that of man and, indeed, excavations of Neanderthal man have shown a brain size (1600cc) which is greater than that of modern man (1400cc).

Evolutionists have gotten excited about animal intelligence when they were able to show that a chimpanzee can place a stick down an ant hole and bring up ants which are then eaten. Training of chimpanzees has come at great expense and effort, and is based mainly on a sense and reward system (food), and on repetition. Many millions of dollars have been invested over the years to find evidence for the intelligence of primates (Yerkees Primate Center, etc.). Since there are no similar programs for horses or dogs, can one assume that such studies are strictly to obtain evidence for the theory of evolution comparing the similarity of intelligence for all primates? How does the intelligence of the chimpanzee compare to man who can make a germanium chip that can send an ICBM carrying a thermonuclear bomb 5,000 miles away and hit a target within one-half square mile or modern man who can build a 100 story skyscraper or perform delicate brain surgery? On the other hand, chimpanzees are still captured in the wild by placing fruit inside a container. When the chimpanzee sticks its hand inside the container in order to grasp the fruit, it is subsequently captured when it is unable to extract its hand still clenched around the fruit.

In addition to the enormous difference in intelligence between man and other primate species, is the ability of man to function in spiritual dimensions, for example play symphonic music, paint a Mona Lisa or worship God. Figure 7 shows a number of cave paintings and carvings collected from various places ranging in dates from 12,000–33,000 years old. Isn't it interesting that there are no earlier cave paintings from the ancestors of man that are 3 million years old or even 300 thousand years old?

The oldest known authentic human fossils are the Costenedolo fossil (skull) which is believed to be 25,000 years old, and the Olmo fossil (skeleton) which is believed to be 50,000–75,000 years old. A date of 150,000 years ago is the earliest date proposed for "Mitochondrial Eve," the woman who possessed the mitochondrial genome inherited by all humans. mDNA has been used as an evolutionary clock by measuring the mDNA of a person and comparing it to a much older specimen. The mDNA can vary from a mother to child only if a mutation occurs; therefore, analyzing the mDNA from one subject to a much older subject, mutation rates can be established. By this method one can determine the time elapsed between subjects. The occurrence of the 150,000-year-old date depends entirely on how accurately the mDNA mutation rate has been determined. Although earlier studies (Khan and Gibbons, *Science*, 277 p. 177, 1997) proposed the age of Mitocondrial Eve to be 150,000 years, Ross more recently has proposed an earlier age of 50,000 years based on heteroplasmy considerations. (Ross, *Facts and Faith*, v.2, n.1, pp 1-2, 1987).

Is it possible that man is not any older than about 50–70 thousand years? There is no convincing evidence that any species prior to man has painted images, played music on musical instruments, buried its dead or has worshiped a higher being. Primitive sounds by primates could be classified as communication but could hardly be classified as music on the level of Beethoven's 5th Symphony.

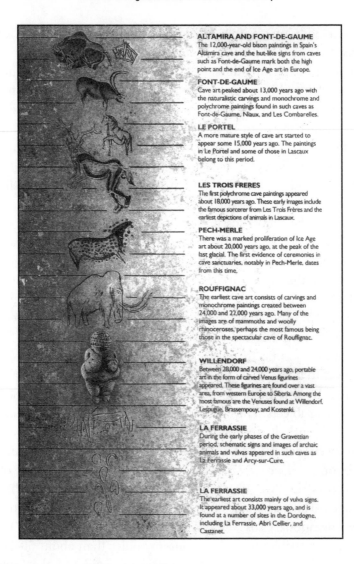

ALTAMIRA AND FONT-DE-GAUME
The 12,000-year-old bison paintings in Spain's Altamira cave and the hut-like signs from caves such as Font-de-Gaume mark both the high point and the end of Ice Age art in Europe.

FONT-DE-GAUME
Cave art peaked about 13,000 years ago with the naturalistic carvings and monochrome and polychrome paintings found in such caves as Font-de-Gaume, Niaux, and Les Combarelles.

LE PORTEL
A more mature style of cave art started to appear some 15,000 years ago. The paintings in Le Portel and some of those in Lascaux belong to this period.

LES TROIS FRERES
The first polychrome cave paintings appeared about 18,000 years ago. These early images include the famous sorcerer from Les Trois Frères and the earliest depictions of animals in Lascaux.

PECH-MERLE
There was a marked proliferation of Ice Age art about 20,000 years ago, at the peak of the last glacial. The first evidence of ceremonies in cave sanctuaries, notably in Pech-Merle, dates from this time.

ROUFFIGNAC
The earliest cave art consists of carvings and monochrome paintings created between 24,000 and 22,000 years ago. Many of the images are of mammoths and woolly rhinoceroses, perhaps the most famous being those in the spectacular cave of Rouffignac.

WILLENDORF
Between 28,000 and 24,000 years ago, portable art in the form of carved Venus figurines appeared. These figurines are found over a vast area, from western Europe to Siberia. Among the most famous are the Venuses found at Willendorf, Lespugue, Brassempouy, and Kostenki.

LA FERRASSIE
During the early phases of the Gravettian period, schematic signs and images of archaic animals and vulvas appeared in such caves as La Ferrassie and Arcy-sur-Cure.

LA FERRASSIE
The earliest art consists mainly of vulva signs. It appeared about 33,000 years ago, and is found at a number of sites in the Dordogne, including La Ferrassie, Abri Cellier, and Castanet.

Figure 7.
Earliest Known Paintings and Carvings.

(Illustration on p. 107 from *The First Humans* [*The Illustrated History of Humankind*, V.1] by Geran Burenhult, general editor. Copyright 1993 by Weldon Owen Pty. Ltd./Bra Bocker AB.) Reprinted by permission of Harper Collins Publishers Inc.

D. Discussion and Conclusions Concerning the Origin of Man

Darwinian evolutionists have hurt their cause by overplaying the scientific merits of their theory. There is convincing evidence for the evolutionary process linking closely related species; however, the evidence is lacking to support the proposal that one kind of species can evolve to an entirely different kind of species. Some evidence is available to support the proposed linkages between reptiles and mammals and between reptiles and birds. The weakness in these proposals lies in the inability to provide the necessary intermediate species, and to provide an argument to satisfy the profound physiological changes (respiratory system, cardiovascular system, reproductive system, etc.) that take place in proceeding from e.g. reptiles to birds (see Denton, *Evolution: A Theory in Crisis*, pp. 143-232, 1986). Such proposals are not unreasonable, but lack substantiating evidence. Where the theory of Darwinian evolution is weakest is at the beginning of the proposed evolutionary cycle linking the first cell to the first organism to the first species. Where is the evidence that the first cell came about by chance and then proceeded by defined biochemistry and molecular biology to produce the first species?

The conclusion from all of the above evidence is that man is definitely a most unique species, not comparable in any way—except similarities in DNA and morphology—to any other species. It has been shown that the DNA of primates is 95 percent (earlier thought to be ~98.3–98.7 percent) similar to that of man[3] and that the morphology of man and the ape is quite similar as seen in Figure 8. It seems obvious, however, based on the intellectual, emotional and spiritual differences between man and other primates that something very dramatic

---

3. It has been reported that DNA determinations are accurate for 50,000-100,000 year old specimens (Nigel Williams, Science 269, 923, 1995).

happened in between the time that earlier primates and man found themselves inhabiting the earth side by side. This very dramatic something, that is also consistent with the Bible, is that after the appearance of plants, marine life and birds, and animals, man appeared. Therefore it is reasonable to suggest that at the time of the appearance of man, God breathed into man a soul, a

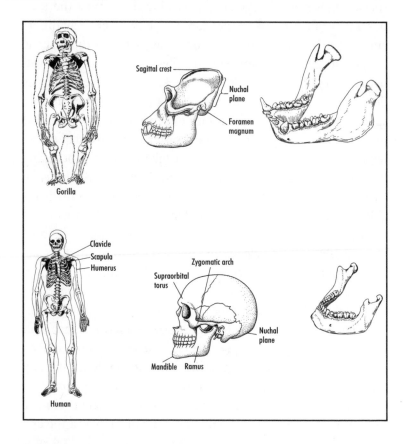

Figure 8.
Morphology of the Ape and Man.

From Marvin Harris, *Culture, People, Nature,* 7/e. Longman, seventh ed. pp. 27-31, 1997. Published by Allyn and Bacon, Boston, MA. Copyright by Pearson Education. Reprinted by permission of the publisher.

spirit and an intellect (making man in the image and likeness of God) and making him very different from his predecessors having similar morphology and DNA. Man is clearly unlike any other species on the face of the earth. Just as Hawking and Einstein have attributed a super intellect as the originator of the universe, it should be reasonable to suggest that a super intellect (e.g. God) is also responsible as the originator of man in all of his uniqueness. Is there any other explanation?

Scientific creationists have had to maintain a young earth model (6,000-10,000 years old) in order to correspond to the early age of the appearance of man (their interpretation of the Bible) when actually the appearance of the earth and the appearance of man are separated by 4 billion years. Scientific creationists do not want to admit to an old earth (4 billion years) because they fear that there is sufficient time for evolution to take place. The first example of life (bacteria) appeared approximately 200-300 thousand years after the earth cooled enough to sustain life. Is this enough time to generate a cell by chance from a primordial soup? The answer to this question is no and supporting evidence for this answer will be presented in the next section when the formation of the cell will be discussed in detail.

Scientific creationists believe that the concept of evolution is contrary to biblical teaching, and they believe that to accept evolution is to be unfaithful to the teachings of their faith. Unfortunately, they do not seem to realize that after creation of the first species, evolution could be God's way of producing many other species to populate the earth. Even scientific creationists admit to the validity of the process of microevolution. A question to be addressed is: How many microevolutionary changes does it take to make a macroevolutionary change?

There is very strong morphological and DNA evidence to trace the evolution of one species or genus to another. The process has been established: however, what is not known is (1) how far back in the evolutionary process can one go? And

(2) how does man fit into this picture? As for question (1) we do not know how far back one can go but morphologically it is easy to see, for example, how the present-day dog (canine) has evolved from a common ancestor of the coyote or wolf, or maybe even further back in time from a common ancestor of the bear. The physiological differences are also comparable. It would not be unreasonable to suggest that God created first marine life and birds during the fifth period of creation which would be consistent with the Cambrian Explosion 540 million years ago, and from these species have evolved thousands of other species. Also, it would not be unreasonable to suggest that God created during the sixth period of creation, basic animal types from which evolved thousands of other animals, some of which are already extinct. The proposition that many different animal types are related by DNA and some common physiological traits is consistent with the theory of macroevolution; however, such evolutionary processes have not been verified by sound scientific investigation and therefore must not be referred to as "fact." Nevertheless, Miller *(Finding Darwin's God)* maintains: "We can no longer explain away the necessity of a creator than we can explain away the process of evolution as God's way to produce new species." Also, theologian John F. Haught had this to say: "God is the deepest thing happening in a Darwinian universe that is unfinished on its evolutionary path to the future" (*Deeper than Darwin: The Prospects of Religion in the Age of Evolution*, Westview Press, 2003).

With respect to question (2) "what about man?", it is suggested that man was a special creation using the same building blocks (proteins, carbohydrates, etc.) and the same mechanisms (DNA, chromosomes, metabolic reactions, physiology, etc.) as used previously in forming other animal species. The big difference is that although the evolutionary process that may have produced the ape from a previous species is still in effect, God directly intervened and placed a soul, a spirit and an intellect into the species Homo sapiens that we call man. To deny that man is extraordinarily different intellectually, spiritually and emotionally from previous species similar in morphology and DNA from other primates requiring a special event to explain these differences, shows a bias not based on sound logic.

Nonetheless, the overall conclusion is that microevolution, as a process for species change, is well established. Evidence for common ancestry back to phyla (macroevolution: species → genus → family → order → class → phyla) is circumstantial and unproven, but not without merit. All scientific evidence still properly labels macroevolution as a theory, not a fact. However, the time has come to realize that the theory of limited macroevolution does not violate the teachings of the Bible. Evolution as a phenomenological process is well established. The only question remaining is how far back does it go? Do species go back in the evolutionary process to a previous species, to phyla, to the first cell or to the big bang with God's direction every step of the way? There is no way of knowing. However, after the Cambrian Explosion, for evolution to proceed from phyla to species with God intervening at the appearance of animals and man (sixth day of creation) in a directed evolutionary process, seems not to violate the teachings of the Bible, although convincing scientific evidence is not available.

In the past, evolutionists have been referred to as godless evolutionists or atheistic evolutionists. There are today a considerable number of committed, born-again Christians with a strong scientific background who believe that there is considerable evidence to support Darwinian evolution. There are scientists who have studied the scientific issues in depth and have not accepted hearsay testimony from those who are simply repeating what they heard from someone else who has not studied the issues. These scientists, who believe in Darwinian evolution, believe that the glory of God is further manifested as his creation continues to unfold in the evolutionary process. Each time a new species appears as a result of a branching process from an ancestor, can be considered an opportunity to marvel once again at the result of God's ongoing creative process which started with the first cell. This is not an unreasonable position when one makes allowances for biblical creation, namely, the appearance of plant life, marine life and birds on the fifth day (Cambrian Explosion) and the appearance of animals and man on the sixth day involving a direct creative act by God. Unlike animals, man was created in the image and likeness of God and is different from the animals that appeared much earlier. This type of Theistic evolution is not inconsistent with the nature of God, the teachings of the Bible and recent scientific findings.

Just as in the seventeenth century it was difficult to accept the theory that the earth revolves around the sun because of its perceived incompatibility with biblical teaching, creationists should not shut down their reasoning about evolution because they have been taught over the years that the process of evolution is anathema. Science was never meant to be the enemy of religion, but rather its helpmate. Science is concerned with the "how" of creation whereas religion is concerned with the "who" and the "why" of creation. Science can be a big help in understanding who we are and from whence we have come.

Man Reveals the Glory of Science
Science Reveals the Glory of Nature
Nature Reveals the Glory of its Creator

Although evolution can explain the appearance of closely related species, it cannot explain the appearance of the first cell. There is absolutely no evidence to suggest that the most simplistic first cell formed as a matter of chance, especially when one considers the extreme complexity of the first cell even at a very early stage. The next chapter addresses this question in some detail.

III. The Origin of Life

If it could be demonstrated that any complex organ existed which could not possibly have formed by numerous successive, slight modifications, my theory would absolutely break down.

Charles Darwin

A. Introduction

STRICTLY SPEAKING THERE IS A DIFFERENCE BETWEEN Darwinian or neo-Darwinian evolution and the origin of life. Darwinian evolution involves living organisms with a functional genetic code and assumes the existence of cells without explaining where they came from. The origin of life is concerned mainly with providing a reasonable explanation for the appearance of the first cell. Many Darwinian evolutionists and others do not make a distinction between the two concepts, holding the position that both are a result of non-directed chemical phenomena (chance).

Unquestionably, most people consider the most significant report since Darwin's book supporting evolutionary theory, is the report by Urey and Miller in 1953 which proposed a pathway to explain the origin of life. This report showed that hydrogen (H_2), ammonia (NH_3), methane (CH_4) and water (H_2O) reacted in the presence of an electrical spark to form amino acids which are the building blocks of proteins essential to all forms of life. The experiment was designed to mimic the composition of the early atmosphere 4 billion years ago reacting with the help of an electrical spark (mimic for lightning) as the energy source. Hence, the conclusion proposed is that a natural explanation for the origin of the molecules necessary for life is now available. Figure 9 shows how the experiment was carried out.

The Urey-Miller report is indeed very interesting but cannot account for the origin of life for many reasons. Only four of these reasons will be presented here.

1. The gas phase reaction of H_2, NH_3, CH_4 and H_2O has been shown to form alpha amino acids (in low yield), which are solids (that are soluble in water) and would fall into the ocean or on ground. No further reaction is expected on solid ground and if the amino acids would fall into the ocean, the concentration ($<10^{-7}M$) would be too dilute for the formation of proteins. Since the formation of proteins from amino acids results in the elimination of water, then carrying out the reaction in the ocean (or a small ditch) where water is in large excess would be quite detrimental to the formation of proteins. This is because the reaction of amino acids to form proteins is a reversible reaction eliminating water and therefore, by the law of mass action, would be expected to reverse itself in the presence of a large amount of water as depicted by equation 5.

$$\underset{NH_2}{\overset{H}{R}}\ \overset{O}{\underset{}{C}}\ \overset{\|}{C}\ OH + H\ \overset{H}{N} - \underset{R}{\overset{H}{C}} - \overset{O}{\overset{\|}{C}} - OH \underset{}{\overset{-H_2O}{\rightleftharpoons}} \underset{NH_2}{\overset{H}{R}}\ C - \overset{O}{\overset{\|}{C}} - N - \underset{R}{\overset{H}{C}} - \overset{O}{\overset{\|}{C}} - OH \rightarrow Protein$$

(eq. 5)

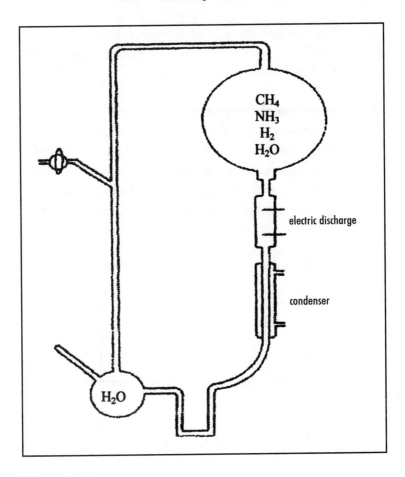

Figure 9.
Urey Miller Experiment
Devised to mimic conditions on planet earth 4 billion years ago.
Water in lower left bulb is vaporized and allowed to mix with NH_3,
CH_4 and H_2 in the upper right bulb which then passes through an
electric discharge. The products and unreacted gases then pass
through a condenser for cooling purposes and then the products
are collected in the lower left bulb containing the water. After one
week a small amount of several amino acids was detected.

The low concentration of amino acids in the ocean plus the reversibility of the reaction speak strongly against this method for the formation of proteins.

2. The formation of alpha amino acids by the Urey-Miller method produced a racemic mixture of amino acids (equal amounts of D and L isomers). A biologically active protein in most cases should contain only one of the isomers (D or L) of the mixture. If both D and L isomers are present, they will both react and the resulting protein will not exhibit the same biological activity as when only one isomer is present.

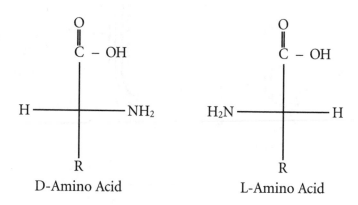

D-Amino Acid   L-Amino Acid

The two amino acids shown above are mirror images of each other and although these compounds have the same number and kinds of atoms, they are not superimposable, therefore do not have the same configuration and therefore are not identical compounds. Only 20 of the more than 80 naturally occurring amino acids are biologically active, and of this 20, only those of the proper configuration (D or L) can be used for protein synthesis.

It is possible to resolve D and L isomers using specific clays. Such reactions are very sensitive and require great care with respect to purity of reagents, temperature, etc. The amino acid isomers would still have to be separated in order to produce pure products from a very impure goo and then proceed further to form proteins. Could the thousands of proteins needed to support life, each having a different structure, be produced by such a method? And then when you have a complex mixture of impure compounds, how does this translate to a living cell containing thousands of other different kinds of compounds?

3. There are many other amino acids that are formed that are not alpha amino acids. When these compounds react along with the alpha amino acids that are present, the resulting proteins will not be biologically active. There are also other compounds (that are not amino acids) formed in the Urey-Miller experiment (e.g. carboxylic acids, ketones, etc.) that will react with amino acids and therefore interfere with the formation of biologically active proteins.

4. Many other types of compounds (lipids, carbohydrates, phosphate, amine bases, etc.) are needed to form a cell, all under very specific conditions. In addition, forming DNA and RNA would also be impossible since the sequence of nucleotides necessary to form self-replicating DNA or RNA is further complicated by the fact that a nucleotide is composed of several components which are not interchangeable. In addition, the DNA chain consists of thousands to millions of nucleotide units which exist in a double stranded helix form, whereas the RNA chain consists of 60 to several thousand nucleotide units which exist normally in a single stranded form. All nucleotide units must be arranged in a specific fashion in order for DNA and RNA to function properly.

Evolutionists maintain that life began in an oxygen-free atmosphere in order to explain why intermediate organic compounds (amino acids, proteins, amine bases, etc.) were not destroyed by oxidation over the long period of time necessary for life to begin. If this is true, then the same organic compounds would have been destroyed by ultraviolet radiation from the sun because without oxygen, there would not have been a protective ozone layer. Perhaps even more important is the fact that today it is no longer believed that the earth's early atmosphere was the composition studied by Urey and Miller, therefore their results (for which they received the Nobel Prize in chemistry) have lost their significance with respect to explaining the origin of life.

Other arguments can be made against the Urey-Miller experiment as an explanation for the origin of the molecules necessary for life. However, even if one could make a peptide with a few amino acid molecules, this is a far cry from the preparation of the thousands of much higher molecular weight compounds that are found in a simple animal cell.

B. The Cell
The Concept of "Probability Exclusion"

It is clear that anthropology is argumentative and ambiguous at best in explaining the origin of man. However, the origin of man is not nearly as fundamental a question as the origin of life, and if life originated by intelligent design of the first cell[4], then the answer concerning the origin of man is not nearly as important as previously thought. Although the origin of man is still somewhat confused, the origin of life is less so because the formation of the simplest unit of life, which is the cell, can be evaluated on a mathematical probability basis. Although an

---

4. It is conceivable that all of the information needed for the creation of life was embodied in the initial design of the universe.

early cell prototype would have been much less complicated than the present day cell, still the complexity would have been far beyond that which could have been formed by chance. Probability calculations clearly show that it is impossible for a cell to have evolved by chance. That leaves only one other explanation—that it was created by intelligent design.

Now let's spend some time establishing the integrity of the above statement. For example, let's consider the make up of a cell and its chemistry. One of the questions to be asked is, What is the probability of forming the chemical compounds contained in the cell that are necessary to produce the chemistry in the different organelles of the cell? One might suggest that the many large molecules found in a cell could possibly have been assembled stepwise over a long period of time in the presence of certain agents that can give directiveness to the forming structures. However, it is clear that thousands of such structures could not come about under the many restrictions that exist with respect to forming such structures in a concerted fashion in a cell.

Figure 10 shows a typical animal cell. Cells are the atoms of biology, the fundamental unit of life. The cell is composed of several organelles such as the ribosomes, the lysosomes, the mitochondria, etc. All organelles are carrying out incredibly complex chemistry which is all interrelated so that the overall effect is to produce and sustain life. The nucleus contains DNA, RNA, etc., that are part of the chromosomes which provide billions of bits of information that dictate the specific and precise chemistry needed for the formation and operation of the kidneys, liver, pancreas, brain, etc. The walls of the cell are made up of lipids in which are imbedded certain protein molecules which determine what is allowed to leave and enter the cell. There are more than 100 trillion cells in the human body (30 billion alone in the brain) and each cell contains at least three billion bits of data contained within the DNA (there are approximately 155,000 cells in every square centimeter of human skin.) If a cell could be enlarged billions of times, it would resemble a city divided into neighborhoods, shopping areas, manufacturing areas, commercial business areas, etc., each involved in thousands of specific activities that result in its functioning as a viable city.

C. Alpha Chymotrypsin

It would be impossible to consider the entire known chemistry of a cell; however, it would be instructive to consider at least one important biological reaction, the cellular digestion of macromolecules such as proteins. When proteins are

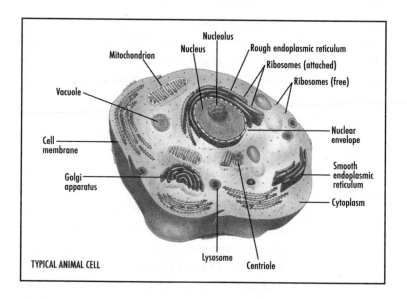

Figure 10.
An Animal Cell Showing All of Its Organelles.

(From *Biology* by Kenneth R. Miller, Ph.D. and Joseph Levine, Ph.D. p. 89, 1995 by Prentice Hall.) Used by permission of Pearson Education, Inc., Upper Saddle River, NJ.

hydrolyzed (react with water) they form amino acids. In order for this hydrolysis to take place rapidly enough, an enzyme catalyst is necessary. There are about 40 enzymes in the lysosomes that fall into several categories, one of which is called proteases. An example of a protease is alpha chymotrypsin which is synthesized in pancreatic cells and secreted, via a pancreatic duct, into the duodenum. Alpha chymotrypsin contains 241 consecutive amino acids taken from the pool of the 20 essential amino acids. The probability of assembling the 241 amino acids in a precise predetermined sequence by chance is given by equation 6.

$$\text{Probability} = 20^{-241} = \sim 10^{-313} \qquad \text{(eq. 6)}$$

Therefore there is one chance in 10^{313} chances that the precise assemblage of amino acids to form alpha chymotrypsin could take place if one added one amino acid at a time. Because one chance in 10^{50} chances is considered by mathematicians to be zero, it is clear that alpha chymotrypsin cannot be formed by chance. If one did not find this result convincing, remember that there are approximately 2,000 enzymes in the cell, thousands of different proteins, carbohydrates, lipids, DNA, RNA, etc. Sir Fred Hoyle, an agnostic evolutionist, reported probability calculations that showed one chance in $10^{40,000}$ chances to form the 2,000 enzymes needed for a cell to function, each enzyme doing a specific job. (F. Hoyle, *Steady State Cosmology Revisited*, University College, Cardiff, 1980). To suggest that all of the compounds, needed to produce a cell could be formed by chance when the probability of forming just one enzyme by chance is zero, would indeed be an impossible position to defend. Of course it is true that probability calculations do not take into consideration factors such as preferential assemblage due to the effect of other substrates, etc. On the other hand, this and other factors do not change the conclusion of the calculations since there are so many other very sensitive conditions that lessen the probability of protein formation from amino acids (e.g. purity of combining materials, temperature, etc.). It is clear that a cell could not form spontaneously and without any direction.

It is interesting, if not amazing, that alpha chymotrypsin must be in a certain conformation (i.e., special spatial arrangement) in order for it to function as a catalyst in protein hydrolysis. This very long straight chain molecule must fold in a very specific way in order to provide a cavity just the right size for a protein molecule to fit and be activated for attack by a water molecule (hydrolysis). In Figure 11 the cavity (shaded area) can be seen which holds the protein molecule by binding it to the specific amino acids in the backbone of the alpha chymotrypsin cavity. Figure 12 shows in more detail exactly what is happening (the mechanism of reaction) on a molecular and electronic basis. The outer shaded area shows the backbone of the cavity containing the amino acids: aspartic acid, histidine, serine and glycine which hold the protein in place for hydrolysis. In this way hydrolysis of the protein becomes at least a thousand times faster than if the enzyme was not present. Reactions of this type must be very rapid in order to meet the rigid requirements of cellular and metabolic reaction rates. No attempt will be made to explain the electron transfers (arrows) involved in the individual steps which result in the formation of the protein hydrolysis products. It is only important to recognize that very precise and involved electron and molecular interactions are necessary for successful reaction to take place.

A more mundane way to view probability is to consider disassembling a watch containing 100 moving parts and putting the parts in a box. If one then shakes the box, how long will it take to reassemble the watch? Table 4 gives the results of 1, 10 and 10,000 watches.

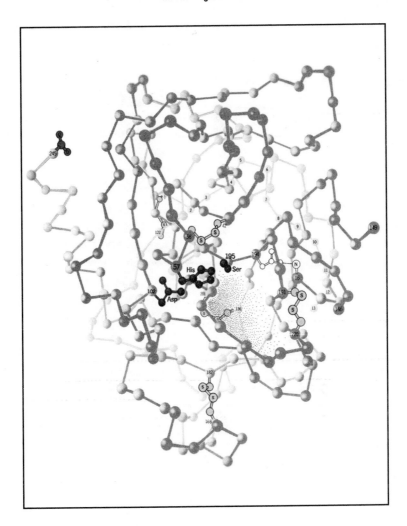

Figure 11.
Alpha Chymotrypsin
This molecule is in a special conformation that provides a cavity to hold a protein molecule leading to accelerated hydrolysis.

(From *Organic Chemistry*, 6th ed., p. 1237, by Robert Thornton Morrison and Robert Neilson Boyd, Copyright (c) 1992, 1987, 1983, 1973, 1966, 1959 by Prentice-Hall, Inc.) Reprinted by permission of Pearson Education, Inc., Upper Saddle River, NJ.

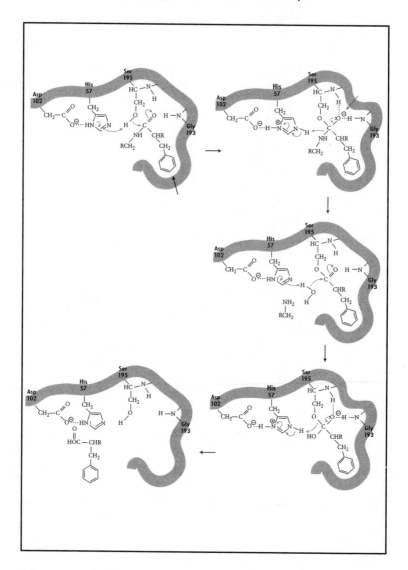

Figure 12.
Proposed Mechanism for Alpha Chymotrypsin Catalyzed Hydrolysis of the Peptide Bond.

(Bruice, Paula Yurkanis, *Organic Chemistry*, 1st ed., 1995, Prentice Hall.)
Reprinted by permission of Pearson Education, Inc., Upper Saddle River, NJ.

Table 4.

The Probability of Reassembling a Watch from Its Component Parts

No. of Watches	No. of Parts	Probability of Assemblage
1	100	10^{-158}
10	1,000	$10^{-1,580}$
10,000	1,000,000	$10^{-158,000}$

Since one chance in 10^{50} is considered zero, and since 10,000 watches would resemble more than one watch the moving parts in a cell, it is clear that there is no chance to assemble 10,000 watches (or even one watch for that matter) from its component parts. Therefore, there is no chance to assemble a much more complex entity such as a cell from its component parts. The cell, and what it does, is unquestionably the single most complex machine in the universe.

D. HEMOGLOBIN

Most enzymes like alpha chymotrypsin are proteins. Let us consider the composition of hemoglobin, a common protein that is very important in the functioning of the human body. When the heme group (A) in Figure 13 is imbedded in the cavity of the protein globin, the resulting product is referred to as myoglobin (B). Myoglobin consists of four polypeptide chains: two alpha chains consisting of 141 amino acids and two beta chains consisting of 146 amino acids. When four myoglobin molecules combine, hemoglobin (C) is formed.

Hemoglobin has a molecular weight of 64,458 and contains 574 amino acids in four separate polypeptide chains in its quaternary structure. The chemical composition of hemoglobin is

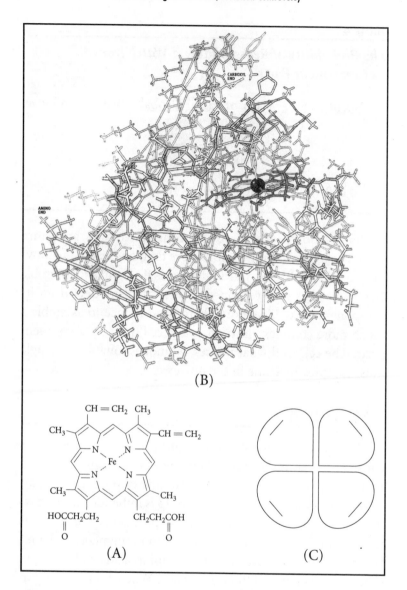

Figure 13.
Structures of (A) Heme, (B) Myoglobin, (C) Hemoglobin.

(Gray and Haight, *Basic Principles of Chemistry*, W.A. Benjamin Inc., pp. 440-441, 1967). Reproduced by permission of Professor Harry Gray.

given in Table 5. It is important to note that the sequence of amino acids in hemoglobin and other proteins varies considerably from species to species.

Table 5.

Amino Acid Distribution in Hemoglobin

Amino-Acid	Number of Units
Glycine	36
Alanine	68
Serine	31
Tyrosine	30
Proline	25
Valine	56
Isoleucine	1
Leucine	69
Phenylalanine	28
Threonine	14
Trytophan	4
Cystine	5
Methionine	6
Asparagine	47
Glutamine	29
Arginine	12
Histidine	32
Lysine	43
Amide N*	38

*includes Aspartic and Glutamic acids

(Adapted from C.U.M. Smith, *Molecular Biology*, p: 109, (q.v. David Foster, *The Philosophical Scientist,* Dorset Press, New York, p. 80, 1985).

The probability of forming hemoglobin by chance is 20^{-574} or one chance in 10^{746} chances. This very intricate hemoglobin structure provides an iron atom (Fe) in heme which coordinates with oxygen (O_2) and becomes the carrier of oxygen to all parts of the body. Myoglobin stores oxygen in muscle tissue. Oxygen coordinated to iron in heme that is not attached to a globin molecule does not function in the body as an oxygen carrier.

It has been found that when one amino acid in hemoglobin is out of place (i.e., when one valine is substituted for one glutamate) in the 574 amino acid system, the disease sickle cell anemia results. Thus the sequence of amino acids in a protein and the conformation of proteins are very sensitive and have been shown to be crucial in the proper functioning of proteins. The function of hemoglobin represents only one of thousands of different delicate processes in operation in the human body. Many of these processes are coordinated and are dependent on each other. For example, cystic fibrosis is a result of cellular malfunction when an ion channel formed in the cytoplasm cannot make its way to the cell surface; and muscular dystrophy results as a malfunction of a molecule that should help to organize the interior of muscle cells. (Lodish et al, *Molecular Cell Biology*, 3rd ed., Scientific American Books, W. Freeman and Co., p. 9, 1995).

E. Vitamins and Trace Minerals

Another crucial process in the proper functioning of the human body is the involvement of vitamins. There are water-soluble and fat-soluble vitamins that, if not present in proper amounts, will result in various fatal diseases. Thus many of the biochemical processes involved in the human body require certain compounds called vitamins which function in very specific ways in order to provide the crucial help needed for successful reactions. Vitamins are yet another crucial way that demonstrates the incredible complexity of the physiology of human life. Some vitamins can be synthesized in the human body and some have to be obtained from food. Also, some vitamins can be synthesized internally by certain species; for example, vitamin C can be synthesized internally by certain mammals, but not by primates.

Tables 6 and 7 list the essential water-soluble and fat-soluble vitamins, their function in the human body and the consequences if these vitamins are not present.

In addition to vitamins, another factor is required for the chemistry of the human body to function properly and that is the presence of trace elements. Table 8 lists both nonmetals and metals and provides the importance of their functions. Most of the elements which exist as salts are found in the soil. These salts then become part of the food chain through plants that are ingested. Ross has reported that one of the elements, fluorine, is unique compared to the other elements in that it is formed only on the surface of white dwarf stars. When these stars supernova, fluorine is released into the universe to combine and agglomerate with other elements to form planets. It is also interesting that the delivery of another element in the metabolic system, iodine, takes place through the hormone thyroxin (structure shown below).

Thyroxin

F. Metabolic Processes

So far the physiological importance of only single compounds such as alpha chymotrypsin, hemoglobin, vitamins and elemental salts have been discussed. All of these compounds are involved in complex chemical reactions that determine the physiology of the human body. The biochemistry and molecular biology of metabolic systems speak even more than single compounds to the incredible complexity of human life, thus completely eliminating the possibility that life could be initiated by chemistry that originated by chance.

Table 6.

Some of the Water Soluble Vitamins
Required for Human Nutrition

Name	Dietary Sources	Symptoms of Deficiency
Vitamin C (Ascorbic acid)	Citrus fruits, raw green vegetables	Scurvy, bleeding gums, loosened teeth, swollen joints
Vitamin B1 (Thiamine)	Whole grains; liver, heart; legumes	Beriberi, heart failure, mental disturbance
Vitamin B2 (Riboflavin)	Milk, eggs, liver, yeast, leafy vegetables	Fissures of the skin, visual disturbances
Niacin (Nicotinic acid)	Yeast, lean meat, liver, whole grains	Pellagra, skin lesions, diarrhea, dementia
Vitamin B6 (Pyridoxine)	Whole grains; pork, glandular meats, legumes	Convulsions in infants, skin disorders in adults
Vitamin B12 (Cyanocobalamin)	Liver, kidney, brain by bacteria in gut	Pernicious anemia

(Adapted from Bloomfield, "*Chemistry and the Living Organism*," 2nd ed., John Wiley and Sons, pp. 494-495, 1980). Reprinted by permission of John Wiley and Sons, Inc.

Table 7.

Some of the Fat Soluble Vitamins Required for Human Nutrition.

Name	Dietary Source	Symptoms of Deficiency
Vitamin A (A_1-retinol)	Green and yellow vegetables and fruits, cod liver oil	Night blindness, skin lesions, eye disease (in excess—vitamin A toxicity, hyper-irritability, skin lesions bone decalcification, increased pressure on the brain)
Vitamin D	Fish oils, liver; provitamins in our skin activated by sunlight	Rickets (defective bone formation) (in excess—growth retardation in infants above 2000 I.U. per day)
Vitamin E (Tocopherol)	Green, leafy vegetables	Increased fragility of red blood cells
Vitamin K	Produced by bacteria in the intestines	Failure of coagulation

(Adapted from Bloomfield, *Chemistry and the Living Organism*, 2nd ed., John Wiley and Sons, p. 495, 1980). Reprinted by permission of John Wiley and Sons, Inc.

Table 8.

The Trace Elements.

Element	Function
Nonmetals	
Fluorine	Found in bones and teeth, important in the prevention of dental caries
Selenium	Required for prevention of white muscle disease, part of an enzyme that protects against accumulation of peroxides
Iodine	Required for normal thyroid function, found in thyroid hormone
Silicon	Function unknown
Metals	
Chromium	Lowers blood sugar level by increasing the effectiveness of insulin
Manganese	Essential for the function of several enzymes, bone and cartilage growth, and brain and thyroid function
Iron	Found in hemoglobin and many enzymes
Cobalt	Part of vitamin B12 molecule
Copper	Part of many enzymes essential for the formation of hemoglobin, blood vessels, bone tendons and the myelin sheath
Zinc	Essential for many enzymes, normal liver function and synthesis of DNA
Molybdenum	Required for the function of several enzymes
Vanadium	Function unknown
Tin	Function unknown

(Adapted from, Bloomfield, *Chemistry and the Living Organism*, 2nd ed., John Wiley and Sons, p. 374, 1980). Reprinted by permission of John Wiley and Sons, Inc.

As an example of a single metabolic process, we shall consider first the function of epinephrine as a regulatory hormone (Table 9) which increases the rate of the breakdown of glucose to lactic acid, a most vital process.

Table 9.

Some Hormones That Trigger Response in Target Tissues by Increasing the Level of Cyclic AMP in the Tissue

Hormone	Target Tissue	Response
Thyrotropin	Thyroid	Thyroxin secretion
Luteinizing hormone	Ovary	Progesterone secretion
Epinephrine	Muscle	Glycogenolysis
	Fatty tissue	Fat hydrolysis
	Liver	Glycogenolysis

(Adapted from M.M. Bloomfield, *Chemistry and the Living Organism*, 2nd ed., John Wiley and Sons, pp. 504-5, 1980). Reprinted by permission of John Wiley and Sons, Inc.

Figure 14 shows blood capillary flow through a cell membrane. When epinephrine is released into the bloodstream, it attaches itself to the receptor site on the muscle cell membrane which then causes the enzyme adenyl cyclase to be converted from its inactive form to its active form. Active adenyl cyclase then catalyzes the transformation of ATP (adenosine triphosphate) to cyclic AMP (adenosine monophosphate). The cyclic AMP then functions as the catalyst that converts glycogen to glucose through a series of steps. The next transformation of glucose to lactic acid, known as glycolysis, is shown by three arrows which simply represent a series of reaction steps. In actual fact these three arrows can be defined in some detail in

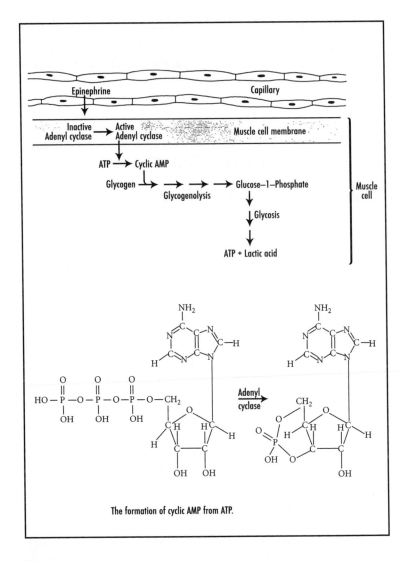

The formation of cyclic AMP from ATP.

Figure 14.
Mechanism of the Effect of Epinephrine on the Conversion of Glucose to Lactic Acid.

(Adapted from Bloomfield, *Chemistry and the Living Organism*, 2nd ed., John Wiley and Sons, pp. 504-505, 1980). Reprinted by permission of John Wiley and Sons, Inc.

Figure 15 to describe the exact chemistry that is involved. In every step from the conversion of D-glucose to lactate, it can be seen that an enzyme is needed to catalyze the transformation. For example, in the first step, the conversion of D-glucose to D-glucose – 6 – P, a phosphorylation reaction, ATP is used as the phosphorylating agent releasing ADP (adenosine diphosphate). This reaction requires the enzyme hexokinase containing magnesium (Mg^{+2}). The most important step in this process is the fourth step catalyzed by the enzyme aldolase which results in the breaking of a carbon–carbon bond converting a six carbon compound (D-fructose –1, 6-di P) to two-three carbon compounds (dihydroxyacetone and glyceraldehyde–3-P). Glycolysis is a complex metabolic process and a nonchemist would not be expected to follow such a process. However, it is important to establish the details and complexity of such processes since these factors speak to the question as to whether such processes could come about by chance.

To further establish the complexity of this process, it would be instructive to concentrate on the fourth step (Figure 15) in order to see exactly how the breaking of the carbon–carbon bond takes place. The first equation in Figure 16 shows D-fructose-1, 6-diphosphate in its noncyclic form being converted to its products (d) and (e) in the presence of the enzyme aldolase. In the mechanistic scheme shown below, the top equation (step 1), D-fructose –1, 6-diphosphate is imbedded in the enzyme catalyst as represented by the three groups to the right of the structure labeled a, b and c. These three entities show the attachment of three amino acids, lysine (a), cystine (b) and histidine (c) which are part of the backbone of the enzyme aldolase which complexes D-fructose –1, 6-diphosphate in order to accelerate the reaction. The series of steps (steps 1-4) simply demonstrate how this complexation causes electron transfer to take place. This explains the bond making and bond breaking which leads to the final products (d and e) while

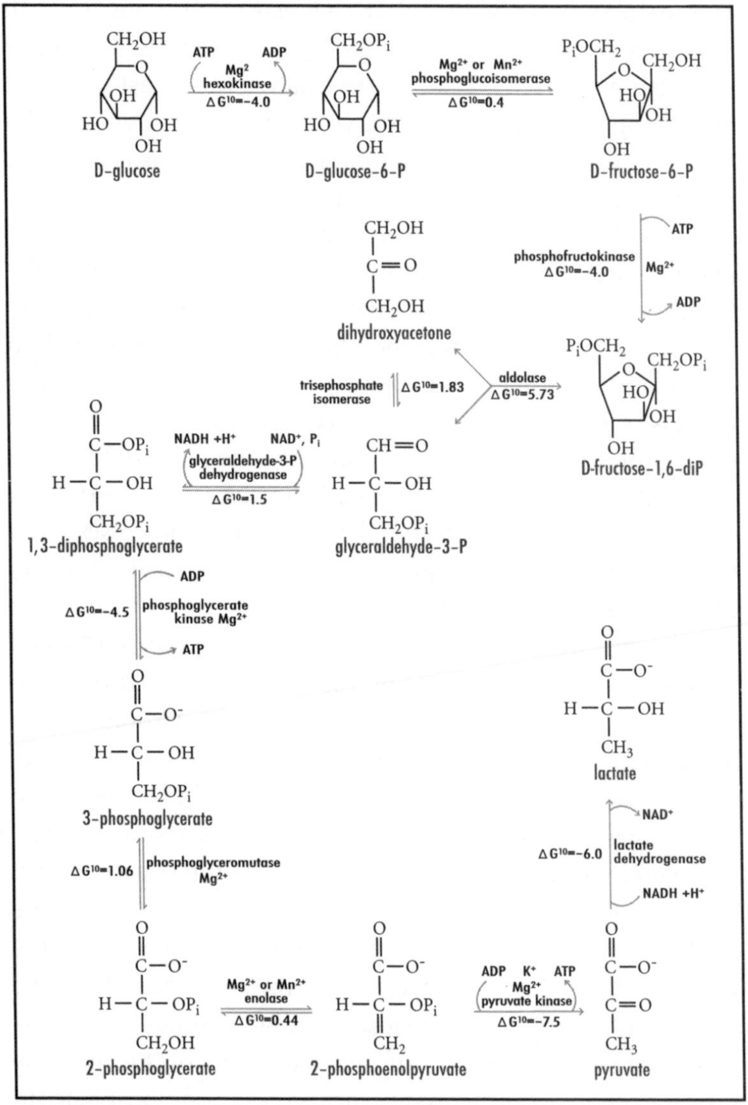

Figure 15.
Glycolysis; the Conversion of Glucose to Lactate (Lactic Acid).

(Bruice, Paula Yurkanis, *Organic Chemistry*, 1st ed., Prentice Hall, p. A-22, 1995). Reprinted by permission of Pearson Education Inc., Upper Saddle River, NJ.

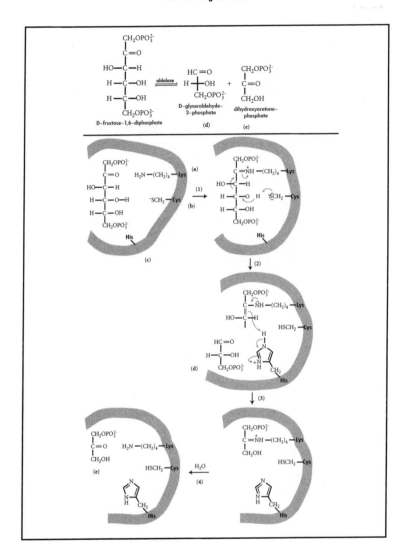

Figure 16.
Mechanism of Aldolase Assistance in the Conversion of a
Six-Carbon Compound to Two Three-Carbon Compounds.

(Adapted from Bruice, Paula Yurkanis, *Organic Chemistry*, Prentice Hall, pp.
1118-1119, 1995). Reprinted by permission of Pearson Education, Inc., Upper
Saddle River, NJ.

regenerating the enzyme aldolase. This series of steps demonstrates only one part of the conversion of glucose to lactate. The preciseness and complexity of the chemistry of these steps speak strongly against this process taking place by chance.

It may be of further interest to consider the fifth step of glycolysis (Figure 15) which involves the conversion of glyceraldehyde–3-P to 1,3-diphosphoglycerate. Not only is an enzyme (glyceraldehyde –3-P dehydrogenase) required for this process, but also a coenzyme, NADH. When reduction takes place, NADH is converted to NAD+. NADH and NAD+ are dinucleotides and contain two different amine bases (nicotinamide and adenine), two sugars (ribose) and two phosphate groups (Figure 17). The remaining steps proceeding to lactate,

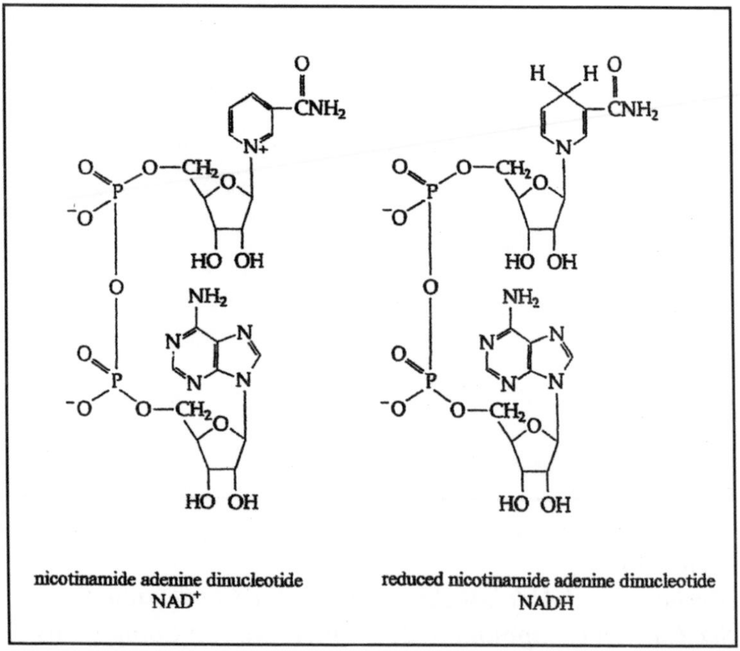

nicotinamide adenine dinucleotide
NAD+

reduced nicotinamide adenine dinucleotide
NADH

Figure 17.
The Chemical Structures of NAD+ and NADH

all involve enzymatic catalysis and involve very complex chemistry. How could so many precise and complicated steps take place by chance? And glycolysis is only one of many metabolic processes that take place in the human body.

G. The Incredible DNA

One of the most exciting and important developments in biochemistry in the twentieth century was the discovery of DNA (deoxyribonucleic acid) and the elucidation of its structure by Watson, Crick and Franklin as a double helix.[5] From this discovery has come a much better understanding of that part of the chromosomes called genes which possess coded information in the form of DNA used to synthesize polypeptide chains. In order to understand better how this happens, it will be necessary to become familiar with the nature of the genetic material, DNA.

DNA belongs to a class of polymers called nucleic acids. These polymers are made up of monomers called nucleotides which themselves consist of three components: an amine base, a five-carbon sugar and a phosphate unit (Figure 18). Nucleotides combine to form dinucleotides which can bond to a complementary dinucleotide through hydrogen bonding (dotted lines) between the amine bases (Figure 19).

Most genes are approximately 1,000 nucleotides long and have a double helix conformation that alternates four amine bases. DNA contains the amine bases: adenine, cytosine, guanine and thymine. RNA has three of the four bases the same. The fourth base, thymine, in DNA is substituted with uracil in

---

5. Normally Rosalind Franklin's name is not included as a codiscoverer of the structure of DNA. This is because she died before the award of the Nobel Prize and therefore did not receive the recognition she deserved. In actual fact, Watson and Crick had no idea of the structure of DNA until they were shown Franklin's crystal structure data (without her permission).

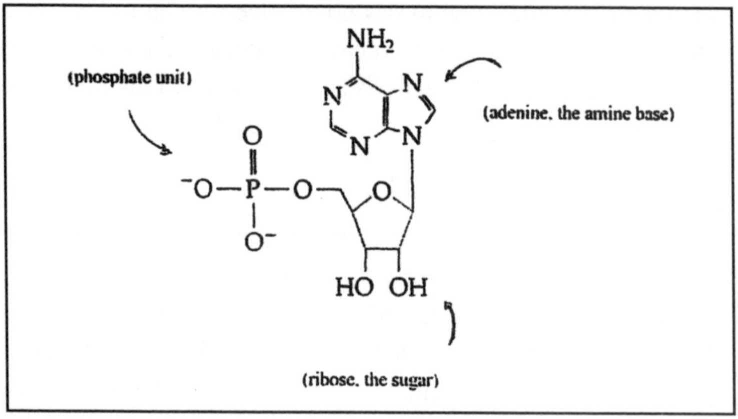

Figure 18.
A Nucleotide

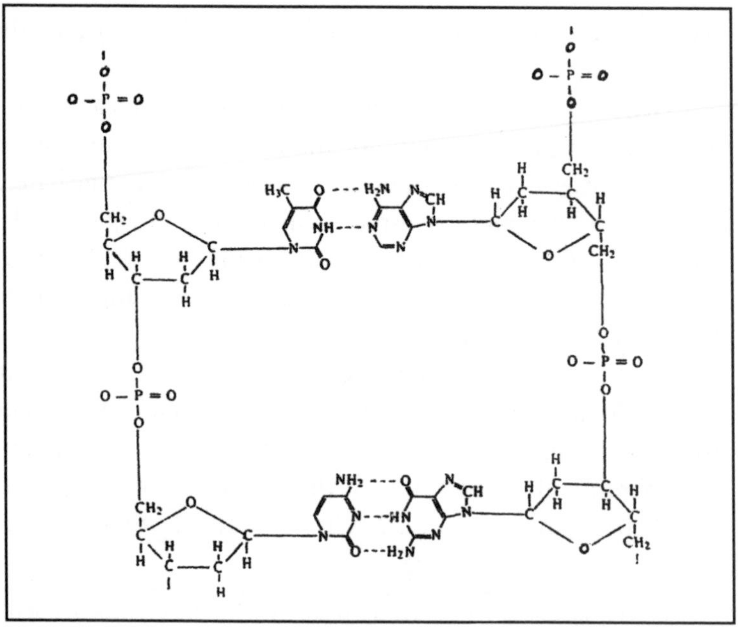

Figure 19.
Two Complementary Dinucleotide Molecules Held Together by Hydrogen Bonding.

RNA. A significant problem in suggesting that DNA and RNA could have been formed by chance in a primordial soup in an oxygen free atmosphere over a long period of time, is that the four amine bases are not stable at the proposed temperatures of the earth even for a short period of time, much less millions of years in the presence of u.v. radiation.

As the dinucleotide is allowed to proceed to form a polynucleotide, a double helix conformation results with hydrogen bonding between the bases holding the two strands of DNA together (Figure 20). When a cell divides, DNA unravels into two strands and then each strand acts as a template for the formation of another identical strand. When completed, two DNA strands are produced, one strand going to each of

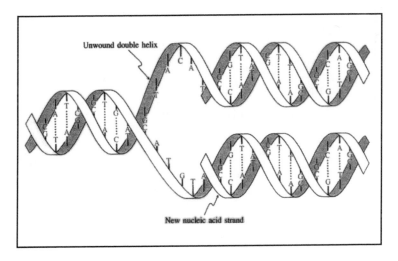

Figure 20.
A Polynucleotide (e.g. DNA).
The double helix initially unwinds to two single strands, each of which is used as a template for reconstruction of the complementary nucleic acid sequence

---

(Vollhardt and Schore, *Organic Chemistry*, 2nd ed., W.H.Freeman and Co., p.1057, 1994). Reprinted by permission from W. H. Freeman and Co.

the divided cells. DNA and RNA can also be used as templates to prepare proteins. The sequence of bases dictates which amino acids are to follow in the synthesis of the protein. The sequence of amino acids can be thought of as words selected from the 20 essential amino acids that make up sentences.

It was shown earlier how two amino acid molecules combine to form a peptide. Figure 21 shows how 9 amino acid molecules combine to form the polypeptide oxytocin. Oxytocin is the messenger hormone required for contraction of the uterus during childbirth and is also responsible for bringing in the

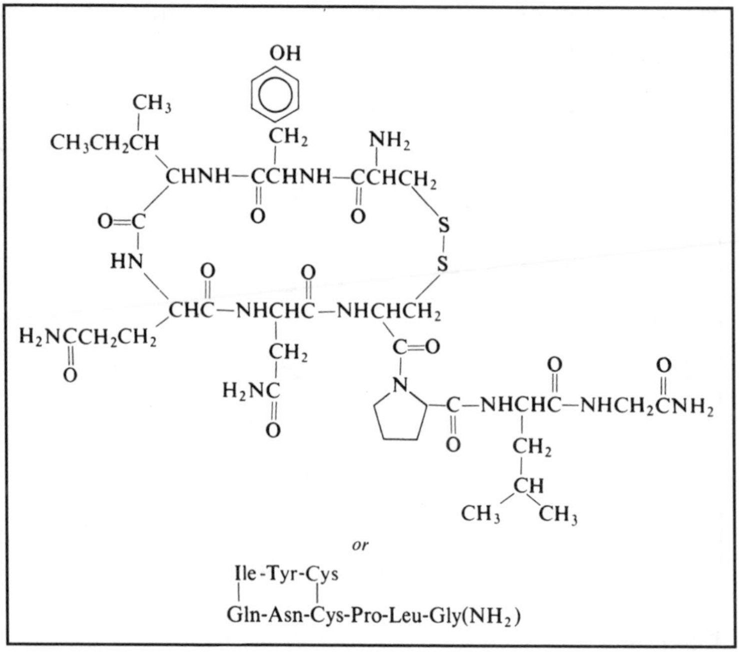

Figure 21.
Oxytocin.

(*Organic Chemistry*, 6th ed. by Robert Thornton Morrison and Robert Neilson Boyd, Copyright © 1992, 1987, 1983,1973,1966,1959 by Prentice Hall, Inc.) Reprinted by permission of Pearson Education, Inc., Upper Saddle River, NJ.

mother's milk. When did chance determine that this was the exact structure needed for such a complex objective?

Proteins also have a specific sequence of amino acids and the chain is usually 100-500 amino acids in length. Specific sequences of amino acids are crucial in producing proteins designated for a specific biochemical purpose and nucleic acids provide the blueprints for the amino acid sequences. Actually the story is much more complicated in that specific enzymes are needed to unzip DNA in order to provide replication of the strands, and the direction of specific amino acids onto the DNA template is dictated by a complicated process. An important question is, How can a particular sequence of amine bases in DNA determine the sequence of amino acids in a protein? The genetic code provides a four letter alphabet consistent with the four amine bases in the DNA backbone. The four amine bases, produced in triplets, can produce 4^3 or 64 different code words called codons. A codon determines the specific amino acid sequence that will determine the structure of the protein. The genetic code consists of 64 codons. It is amazing to realize that such an intricate process is needed in the ribosomes of the cell in order to prepare the thousands of different proteins required to sustain human life. How did the cell know exactly which proteins to synthesize for each of the complex reactions involved in the biochemistry of the human body? Although it is known that DNA is required for the formation of proteins, proteins are required for DNA replication, transcription, translation, etc. The question is, Which came first, proteins or DNA (the chicken or the egg)?

Of course, the chemistry of the ribosomes and lysosomes provide only a small part of all of the chemistry that takes place in a cell. The most recent research has yet to define the complete chemistry of the cell or how the billions of bits of data in the chromosomes are translated into the chemistry of the vital organs. For example, the brain consists of approximately 30 billion nerve cells and each cell is attached to approximately 10,000 connecting fibers which connect to other nerve cells in the brain. These connecting fibers have specific purposes and are essential to specific communication capabilities. Such a network of fibers is more complex than the extremely complex communications network that exists at NORAD for the detection and deployment of nuclear missiles.

Table 10 lists only a few of the vital systems where chemistry is dictated by the information contained in the chromosomes.

Table 10.

Interdependence of Biochemical Processes

1. the brain	6. eyesight
2. the kidneys	7. lymph nodes
3. the liver	8. reproductive organs
4. the endocrine system	9. antibody action
5. the heart	10. muscle response

When liver chemistry fails, all other organs and biochemical processes shut down. Therefore it can be seen that most of the chemistry that takes place in the human body is dependent on the chemistry being produced in multiple organs simultaneously.

In May 2003 an extraordinary scientist, who knows a great deal about DNA and its ability to make proteins, gave a lecture entitled "Faith and the Human Genome" at an ASA meeting televised by the University of California. The man was Francis Collins, director of the Human Genome Institute, who is also a committed Christian. Dr. Collins and his research team have shown that the human genome has been assembled in a stepwise fashion as one would expect from earlier life species evolving into later life species. His opinion is that the long sought evidence for Darwinian evolution is now available. He believes that each species evolved genetically from a previous species and eventually from a cell. He stated categorically that he could see no way how the formation of a cell could be explained. As a devout Christian, he does not see any problem with this interpretation, but rather only marvels at the complex way in which God has produced living organisms.

✳ Dr. Kenneth R. Miller is another example of a committed Christian who is a distinguished scientist and professes a belief in Darwinian evolution. He is a noted cell biologist and is a professor of biology at Brown University. His recent book, *Finding Darwin's God*, is a detailed scholarly analysis of the scientific validity of Darwinian evolution. His position can be summed up with this quote from his book: "There is neither logical nor theological basis for excluding God's use of natural processes to originate species, ourselves included. There is therefore no reason for believers to draw a line in the sand between God and Darwin" (p. 267). Before believers categorically reject or ridicule the concept of Darwinian evolution, they should at least read Miller's book.

It is the opinion of this writer that scientists like Collins and Miller need to be heard, for they present a well thought-out and intelligent case for Darwinian evolution. However, it is also the opinion of this writer that definitive evidence is lacking to support their positions, therefore their positions must be relegated to the position that Darwinian evolution is a theory and not a fact. As will be discussed later, limited macroevolution does not present an insurmountable problem for believers, if one allows for the creation of the first cell, next plant life, and on the fifth day the creation of marine life and birds (Cambrian Explosion) and then on the sixth day the creation of land animals and man.

H. Discussion and Conclusions
Concerning the Origin of Life

All of the examples that have been presented—proposing the impossibility of forming a cell by chance, enzymes and proteins by chance, the impossibility of life being sustained without vitamins and trace elements, the impossibility of generating and sustaining complex metabolic processes by chance and the impossibility of explaining the very complex but necessary function of DNA and RNA in biochemical processes by chance—provide overwhelming evidence that such compounds and processes could not possibly have come about without intelligent direction. Probability calculations show that not even one enzyme (alpha chymotrypsin) could form by chance, much less the 2,000 enzymes and thousands of other proteins, carbohydrates, lipids, DNA, RNA, etc., found in the cell. Since it has been clearly demonstrated that the first cell could not have originated by chance, it is somewhat confusing that many people, including some scientists, still hold, even to this day, the theory that life began by chance, a clearly indefensible, if not absurd, position.

Hence the concept of probability exclusion speaks strongly against the validity of the position that life began by a nondirected, impersonal process in which thousands of complex molecules came together to form the first cell.

IV. General Conclusions

ALL OF THE EVIDENCE CONCERNING THE ORIGIN OF THE UNI-verse, the origin of man and the origin of life presented in this discussion provides the basis for the following conclusions:

1. All scientific evidence supports the age of the universe to be ~17 billion years and the origin of the universe to be best described by the big bang theory.

2. All scientific evidence supports the age of planet earth to be ~4 billion years and that marine life and birds appeared 540 million years ago with land animals and man appearing much later. All evidence to date suggests that man appeared approximately 70-120 thousand years ago.

3. Scientific evidence is overwhelming against the position of scientific creationists concerning the age of the earth (6,000-10,000 years old) and the concept of a six 24-hour creation period.

4. Microevolution as a process to explain the evolution of one species to another species similar in morphology and DNA is well established. Limited macroevolution as a process to explain the evolution of one species to another that differs slightly in morphology and DNA is not well established, but is a theory not without merit.

5. Darwinian evolution (all species originated from the same single cell) should not be considered a valid theory because the Cambrian Explosion produced 70 phyla

suddenly and not gradually, over a long period of time, as demanded by Darwin's theory.

6. It is absolutely impossible that the first cell was the result of any process other than that directed by intelligent design since the thousands of highly complex biologically active molecules needed to form the earliest conceivable cell prototype under primordial conditions could not be formed by chance.

7. The most logical theory to explain the origin of the universe, the origin of life and the origin of man, which is supported by all of the scientific evidence, is that the universe, life and man were the result of creation by God. Creation was then followed by evolution of the universe from the time of the big bang to the present time, evolution of life from the creation of plant and animal life to the present time where species of one kind have evolved to other species of a kind similar in morphology and DNA.

The origin of the universe appears clearly to have had its beginning as a result of a supernatural act. Not even the greatest scientists of this day or any other day have provided any valid alternative explanations. Hundreds of billions of galaxies have appeared as a result of the big bang; each galaxy a result of the astrophysics dictated by the originator of the big bang (God). It was not necessary at every juncture involving a new sun or planet that God was directly involved in a creative act, but rather development of the universe has taken place by a plan that God put in place from before the beginning of time.

Likewise, the origin of life (appearance of the first cell) appears to be the result of a supernatural act. It is not necessary that every form of life began by a sovereign act of God (although that is possible), but by the laws of physics, chemistry and molecular biology that God put into place since before the beginning of time. According to the book of Genesis, chapter 1, after the earth, sun, moon, water, land and plants were created, God on the fifth day created the fish of the sea and birds of the air, and on the sixth day he created all manner of land animals and man. This sequence is consistent with scientific findings, if one accepts that a day can be a period of time, e.g., millions of years. It is reasonable to suggest that the appearance of the kinds of creatures listed in Genesis 1:20-23 (marine life and birds) that appeared during the fifth day of creation, is consistent with the Cambrian Explosion (sudden appearance of 70 phyla), and was the result of a creative act. The appearance of land animals and man on the sixth day is consistent with the long periods of time separating the appearance of marine life and birds 540 million years ago (the fifth day of creation) from the land animals 200 million years ago and man 70-120 thousand years ago (on the sixth day of creation). After all of the different kinds of species were created on the fifth and sixth days, it is suggested that many other species similar in nature could have evolved by a limited macroevolutionary process, although substantiating scientific evidence to establish this point is lacking.

Whether or not man evolved from a previous primate species cannot be answered by science at this time. Man may not have evolved from a common ancestor of the ape, but clearly he is related to a common ancestor of the ape as shown by morphology and DNA relationships. However, what does seem to be clear is that a profound change took place between the appearance of the ape and the appearance of man. Such an intellectual, emotional and spiritual difference could be explained only by a sovereign act of a supernatural being. There appears to be little valid scientific, theological or philosophical reasoning to argue against the premise that the universe and life were initiated by God, and that man, although related to previous species biologically, was a special creation by God containing a soul, a spirit, an intellect and a conscience.

In summary, it appears that at our present state of understanding, there are seven separate major creative acts (acts that only can be attributed to an infinite being—God) from the beginning of the universe to the present time. These creative acts are the appearance of: (1) the big bang, (2) the preparation of planet earth for life, (3) the first cell, (4) plant life, (5) marine life and birds, (6) animals and (7) man. Such conclusions are consistent with the teachings of the Bible and with modern scientific findings.

In addition to the major creative acts listed, it is proposed that evolution more extensive than microevolution (limited macroevolution) may have taken place which explains the similarities in morphology and DNA when comparing certain species. In other words, the process of limited macroevolution, is not without merit. However, there are still many unanswered questions concerning macroevolution, particularly with respect to evolution of the cardiovascular system, the respiratory system, the reproductive system, etc. On the other hand, it is clear that the concept of Darwinian evolution, as defined by Darwin, is invalid. Darwinian evolution necessarily involves macroevolution; however, limited macroevolution does not imply Darwinian evolution. Once again, this writer does not see a contradiction in the position that the origin of the universe, life and man are a result of creative acts, whereas the evolution of the universe and the limited evolution of some animal species similar in morphology and DNA are simply the normal result of a process put into effect by the Creator.

There is another explanation similar to and not inconsistent with the one just presented. This explanation has been eluded to throughout this presentation, and although more speculative, cannot be overruled by modern science, theology or philosophical reasoning.

Instead of the seven different creation events mentioned earlier, one can envision the time from the big bang to the present time as just one creation event. It is suggested that, at the time of the big bang, the Creator (God) provided all of the necessary information to account for all of the creation that is described in chapter one of the Book of Genesis. Therefore, each species that has appeared has come about by the direct design of God expressed over time from the big bang to the present time. This interpretation involves not only creation, but also evolution; God directed evolution. The only possible theological problem is that the bible talks about six individual days of creation. However, one can ask the question, what is the difference between six individual days of creation in which the creation process takes place in six discrete periods of time, and a one step creation process in which the order of the six day creation events expressed in the bible is still observed? Since the writer of chapter one of the Book of Genesis knew nothing of the concept of evolution, it is not surprising that he described creation in a series of simple, systematic creation steps. Whatever evolution that takes place is God directed evolution and not Darwinian evolution (production of species by chance).

The latter theory is very similar to the first theory presented in that it does in one step what was proposed earlier to involve seven steps. Certainly God is capable of having programmed all creation before the beginning of time. It is not suggested that once the creation process begins at the moment of the big bang, God is no longer involved. On the contrary, it is envisioned that God continues to hover over his creation like a mother hen hovers over her chicks.

The latter theory has the advantage of satisfying both sides of the creation/evolution debate. The only disagreement is that creationists believe that God is responsible for the appearance of all species, whereas atheists contend that all species are a result of a non directed process. Of course, this book has shown clearly that the origin of the universe and life could not have taken place by chance.

If we argue about the exactness of the description of creation, which we cannot know for certain, we hurt our ability to see the bigger picture. The bigger picture is that all of the scientific evidence tells us that the universe, life and man are the result of a creator to whom we have given the name, God, and that changes (evolution) in the universe, life and man continues by a creator directed process that we do not completely understand.

So what can we conclude?

Creation, yes.
Darwin evolution, no.
Microevolution, yes.
Limited macroevolution by chance, maybe.
Unlimited macroevolution; only if it is directed by God.

Both Julian Huxley and Carl Sagan have said that to believe in God is a cruel hoax! On the other hand, can anyone look at the sky at nighttime and say there is no God? Can anyone look closely at a single flower, or observe a newborn baby, or see a young white man changing a flat tire at nighttime on the interstate highway for an elderly black couple, or watch a teacher work tirelessly and patiently with challenged young students, or watch those who were once affluent give up everything to feed starving children in Africa, South America, India or other parts of the world, or observe a close friend pack up his wife and four young children and leave a promising research career in the Netherlands in order to help start a new university in Botswana, Africa, or have a close friend willingly die in battle in order to protect his comrades and defend the country he loved—can anyone observe all of these things and say there is no God? One can find God, not only by looking up at the sky, or observing the actions of others, but also by being quiet and listening for a still quiet voice that says, "I am the Lord thy God and you are precious in My sight."

This writer is overwhelmed with the evidence that the super intellect of Einstein and Hawking and the originator of intelligent design is none other than the God of the Bible. This writer is also overwhelmed with gratitude for what has happened in my life, for my family, my friends, my church and my country. Without God, who would I thank?

V. Epilogue

IT IS AMAZING THAT MAN CONTINUES TO TRY TO SEPARATE the spiritual from the temporal, although both are essential parts of human life. We do see in this treatment of creation/evolution that creation represents the spiritual and evolution represents the temporal, and that they do cross paths. Should this be so surprising? As we just determined, one cannot account for the universe and life strictly on scientific grounds. Not to allow a Creator to account for that which science cannot, does not seem reasonable.

No amount of posturing or ridicule by evolutionary biologists and others will suffice any longer to challenge the adequacy of the theory of creation to explain the origin of man and the origin of life. It is the opinion of this writer that the resolution of the creation/evolution debate has been hindered by the position of scientific creationists who insist on a 6,000-10,000 year old earth and a 24-hour creation period. Hopefully this book will help to get the debate past this point so that the remaining crucial issues can be moved to the front. Although this book concentrates on only a few issues, this writer believes that these are the most meaningful issues to be discussed in order to arrive at the simplest understanding of a very complex problem.

From a philosophical standpoint it is not reasonable to suggest that the super intellect that is responsible for the origin of the universe is not also responsible for the origin of life. Surely a super intellect that could create the universe would not allow it to stand null and void, and of no use, but would create those conditions that would make the universe meaningful. Scientifically, the examples given clearly demonstrate that life is that which would have to be created by intelligent design. To insist that life originated by chance has been shown to be not just highly unlikely, but impossible. Why would anyone insist, in spite of overwhelming scientific evidence to the contrary, that life originated by chance? The debate concerning creation/evolution has not been entirely a scientific debate, but one involving positions argued by those who will or will not accept God as the creator of the universe and life, possibly because of the profound implications.

VI. Appendix

Questions

1. How did the first cell come into existence, and how could it program itself to produce a feeling, loving human being?
2. Why have we not developed a third arm or an eye behind the head via evolutionary natural selection processes? Certainly these things are needed.
3. Could evolution in 4 billion years produce the information contained in the cells of one body?
4. How were the initial thousands of protein, lipid, carbohydrate, DNA, RNA, etc., molecules formed, simultaneously in the cell (even in the simplest prototype) and how does one explain the simultaneous development of the resulting complex chemistry of such compounds formed in the organelles of the cell?
5. What do probability calculations suggest as to the synthesis of the above compounds and their resulting reactions?
6. Where did the initial information originate that is encoded in the chromosomes that is responsible for all of the complicated, stereospecific syntheses of thousands of compounds and the resulting chemistry needed to produce a living being?
7. How was the first heart produced and how and when did it start beating? Eyesight? Reproductive system? Respiratory system? Brain? Pituitary gland, etc.?

8. All vital organs are necessary for life. Is it reasonable to expect that all of the biochemistry and molecular biology associated with these organs could be synchronized in such an exact way so as to produce life via the thousands of molecular processes that are needed to do so?

9. What is the probability of a total living human being coming about by chance?

10. How can you explain the absence of ancestors for the Ediacara fauna that appeared just prior to the Cambrian Explosion (700 million years ago)?

11. Why is fossil evidence lacking to confirm the theory of Darwinian evolution?

12. Can a specific objective be accomplished if there is not an intelligence directing the effort? How did bees learn to make a honeycomb? By whose direction do birds fly thousands of miles to an exact place to stay for the winter?

13. How does the theory of life explain not just the origin of matter, but also the origin of information?

14. If the very first living animal species was a newborn infant, how did the infant survive without a father and mother and someone to give it food? Could a mature animal species have appeared first?

15. Has anyone noticed that the media refers to evolutionists as "intellectuals" and creationists as "right-wing intellectual lightweights"?

16. Why is it that you can discuss evolution in the classroom as a theory to explain the origin of life but a discussion of the science that leads to the theory of creation is forbidden? Is this not a violation of First Amendment rights?

17. The creation of the universe and plant, animal and human life is the most stupendous scientific accomplishment of all time. Considering the unique complexity of the universe and life required for their existence, is it reasonable to assume that the universe and life appeared by chance when the synthesis of only one biomolecule, such as vitamin B-12, from already available intermediates, required the diligence, vision, ingenuity and supreme efforts of many brilliant chemists over a long period of time?

19. Can anyone explain the mechanistic pathway that describes in detail how evolution began and how it occurs today?

20. How did microorganisms know from the beginning what molecules would need to be assembled in order to produce male and female reproductive systems? Can organisms think and plan? Without a brain?

21. Why is it in China that teachers can speak openly against the theory of evolution in their schools, but cannot speak openly against the government; whereas, in the United States of America teachers can speak openly against the government in their schools, but cannot speak openly against the theory of evolution?

Understanding the
Creation/Evolution Controversy
Order Form

Postal orders: Stillwaters Farm
Box 323
Franklin Springs, GA 30639

Telephone orders: 706-377-2994

Please send *Understanding the Creation/Evolution Controversy*
to:

Name: _____

Address: _____

City: _____ State: _____

Zip: _____ Telephone: (_____) _____

Book Price: $11.95

Shipping: $2.50 for the first book and $1.00 for each additional book to
cover shipping and handling within US, Canada, and Mexico.
International orders add $6.00 for the first book and $2.00 for
each additional book.

Or order from
your local bookstore